DOING BUSINESS WITH GOD

60 Biblical Principles for Leadership, Business & Politics

By Marricke Kofi GANE

DOING BUSINESS WITH GOD

By Marricke Kofi Gane

ISBN: 978-1-909326-06-4

author@marrickekofigane.com

Published by MarrickeGanePublishing

Distributed by Amazon

DEDICATION

To Jehovah God Almighty,

In whom is our being, for who is our glory.

To all good business people,

Your passion possesses the earth and all its fullness.

To every visionary leader,

Through God, may you lead the world as pillars of cloud and fire

To them that exercise Power,

The Kingdom of God is within you, the hope of Glory.

To God

Be praise, glory and all honour forever.

Contents

INTRODUCTION

As long as the world remains, men and women will do business; some will lead organisations and yet still, others will dabble in the obscure world of power.

In Exodus 25:16, God directs Moses to build an ark and then tells him "*...and you shall put into the ark the testimonies which I will give you*"

In Exodus 25:30 God directs Moses to build a table and then tells him "*....and you shall set the showbread on the table before Me always*"

In Exodus 25:37 God directs Moses to build lampstands then tells him "*....and they shall arrange its lamps so that they give light in front of it*"

In all three scenarios above, God asks Moses to build a physical item and subsequently tells him the purpose of the build. The ark is built to house the Ten Commandments; the table, to hold the show bread; and the lampstands, to give light.

Surprisingly in Exodus 27:1-8, God gives Moses a much more detailed plan to build the "altar" but NEVER tells him what purpose the altar will serve.

And therein is the revelation: the physical components of any entity such as office buildings and equipment derive their purpose from the physical use to which they are put. On the contrary, building an altar to God is a purpose in itself – NOT the physical use it is put to.

The same applies to the subject covered in this book; the entire duty of building a business, leading a people, or using political power to change the course of nations; all three are similar to the building of an altar – each has purpose within itself.

Here in this book, the Spirit of God supernaturally unfolds sixty revelatory principles for building a relevant business, exercising extraordinary leadership and engaging meaningful political power.

For the very first time, you are about to read simple verses in the Bible and find in them tremendous revelations that will edify you, those around you and the generations yet unborn where business, leadership and political power is concerned.

The principles in this book have not been arranged according to the order in which chapters appear in the Bible. Rather, I have retained the order in which these insights came to my spirit. Throughout this book and for ease of reading; wherever reference is made singularly to *"business," "leadership"* or *"political power,"* please assume that the principle applies to the other two at all times except explicitly stated otherwise.

It is my genuine hope that this book will speak to you on more than one level.

Marricke Kofi Gane

Author

Principle 1

MOTIVATION… MOTIVATION… MOTIVATION

1 Chronicles 15: 25 – 28

So David, the elders of Israel, and the captains over thousands went to bring up the ark of the covenant of the Lord from the house of Obed-Edom with joy. [26] And so it was, when God helped the Levites who bore the ark of the covenant of the Lord, that they offered seven bulls and seven rams. [27] David was clothed with a robe of fine linen, as were all the Levites who bore the ark, the singers, and Chenaniah the music master with the singers. David also wore a linen ephod. [28] Thus all Israel brought up the ark of the covenant of the Lord with shouting and with the sound of the horn, with trumpets and with cymbals, making music with stringed instruments and harps…

1 Chronicles 16: 1 – 4

So they brought the ark of God, and set it in the midst of the tabernacle that David had erected for it. Then they offered burnt offerings and peace offerings before God. [2] And when David had finished offering the burnt offerings and the peace offerings, he blessed the people in the name of the Lord. [3] *Then he distributed to everyone of Israel, both man and woman, to everyone a loaf of bread, a piece of meat, and a cake of raisins.* [4] *And he appointed some of the Levites to minister before the ark of the Lord, to commemorate, to thank, and to praise the Lord God of Israel:*

Many business owners and leaders have always struggled with the selection of an organisation-wide motivational model that is deemed best.

Just like the human body, we all look different, but the one thing we all have in common is that we all have a skeletal framework which follows a basic structure for every human being. So we have the skull at the top, followed by the vertebral column to which we have all the other vital attachments.

In the same manner, many business and leadership successes are grounded on some basic human and organisational structures, one of which relates to motivation. The problem has been that these basics have never been taught from the Bible, but rather from secular philosophies which result in successes that are as erratic as the humanity that developed them outside of God.

Embedded in the above passage is a simple yet sublimely efficient principle upon which any business entity or institutional and political leadership can develop an effective motivational system. In order to get the best out of such a system you will need to offload one damaging ideology – that motivation is all about money. Genuinely, people only start expecting money to fill the motivational gap when they are not fully experiencing the other features that make up the complete concept of motivation. Now let's talk about these basic structures:

- *1 Chronicles 15: 25*: *The bosses work too*: David was the king, yet he and his senior executives got their hands dirty by going down to Obed-Edom's house to bring up the Ark. Bosses not only need to work, they need to be seen working. This has two effects- firstly, those looking up to you do not feel they are being "used." Secondly, it takes away from those under your leadership any justification whatsoever to be lazy or complacent.

- *1 Chronicles 15: 26*: Notice that David went down to bring up the ark, but only the Levites were permitted to carry it. David and his executives knew their place. The fact you are the manager or the leader does not mean you have to be involved with everything – let those better placed and qualified to get the specific jobs done do it. Allowing people to do what they can do best gives them a sense of being accepted and recognised as a part of a value adding process. No amount of money can match this.

- *1 Chronicles 15: 27*: Notice that David alone did not array himself in the glory on his return. Everybody did. Do not take all the glory or the credit as a leader because the more you share it, the more it is enjoyed and the more you win to your side.

- *1 Chronicles 16: 2*: Following up from above, we observe David blessing the people. In the previous verse he is sharing credit that has been received, but in this verse he is proactively acknowledging the support of the people and showering them with his own praises and recognition.

Here is the most effective way to praise those who support your vision – (i) acknowledge their involvement, (ii) shower them with praise and then (iii) express your positive hope or expectations for future successes together. This is the parallel to David blessing them in the scripture reading above.

In the actual act of blessing a person in the biblical context, you would usually place your hands on them *(acknowledgement)*, then you would speak the blessing over them *(showering with praise)* and then declare what will manifest in their future as a result *(express your future expectations)*.

An example of this would be you saying: "*I recognise that you played an instrumental role in the organisation's success this year* ***(recognition)*** *and I just want you to know we value all your inputs* ***(praise)*** *and I am even more hopeful now, that you'll put in a lot more to better these results in the next year* ***(expectations)***"

- *1 Chronicles 16: 3*: Then comes the part that many have erroneously defined singularly as motivation – that is, monetary rewards or rewards in tangible forms. If you run a business, this refers to emoluments. David distributed bread, but he did not end it there, although he could have. Instead, he also distributed meat and raisins.

- The latter represented a delicacy. In simple terms, if you perform better than expected, let it be reflected in the pockets of the employees or supporters of your vision. It does not mean the organisation has to go bankrupt; neither does it mean you must grab a box of cash and start doling out.

- In fact, I have seen some very wise business leaders who, instead of paying bonuses in cash to employees, invested such monies for their employees and their children. There are positive ways around rewarding employees or vision supporters without necessarily giving cash, but most importantly, do not sit on the profits alone, except it took your sweat alone. Only then are you justified.

- *1 Chronicles 16: 4:* Bringing the Ark back to Israel was the vision. So great was the vision that David was compelled to go down himself. But after the Ark arrived in Israel, he appointed caretakers from the ordinary people. It did not mean that David was out of touch with the Ark. On the contrary, he was always worshiping before it.

What this really means as a motivation tool, is that as a leader and business owner, you need to arrive at the highest level of organisational motivation – to let the people OWN the vision.

Principle 2

IN TIMES OF BLUNTED DISCERNMENT

1 Chronicles 21: 9 – 10

9 Then the Lord spoke to Gad, David's seer, saying, 10 "Go and tell David, saying, 'thus says the Lord: "I offer you three things; choose one of them for yourself, that I may do it to you."'

Let's face it, being a serious Christian with the right godly principles is far likely to make you a more effective leader or business person.

As an individual leader or business person, the sharpness of your discernment and the accuracy of your spiritual receptivity from God will enable you to always see into the future before your competitors or others do.

If you are a leader without spiritual discernment, then your future is quite bleak, because you will be unable to take advantage of the most crucial commodity in any winning formula – knowing what will happen tomorrow before others do, even if in part. This prior knowledge only comes by hearing from God. The reality is that certain conditions need to be in place for one's receptivity to heavenly agenda remains on a cutting edge.

In the passage, we realize that God was speaking to David's seer and not to David himself. Do not forget David was a very godly man and that in spite of his many faults, God still declared him a man after His own heart. On this occasion, however, after a wrong he had committed, God chose to speak to Gad, his seer. The lesson to be learnt here is this – irrespective of how anointed you may be, so long as you are in business or leadership you need to find a prophet or seer who: (i) you will honour and listen to (ii) is a genuine man of God (iii) God can use to communicate to you about your leadership and business and (iv) honours and respects you.

There really is no need to get defensive and by saying "*but I can hear from God myself too*". While this might be true, and is not being disputed or downplayed here, nevertheless, there are times that due to: (i) pressures of work (ii) sin (iii) health problems and (iv) emotional instability, you might not be able to hear properly from God, or He may not be willing to speak to you because of your state.

If you are still arguing within yourself on the point about sin and asking "*well, who said prophets or seers do not sin?*" Well, they might because they are ordinary men too, but you need to remember that "*the gifts and the calling of God are irrevocable*" *(Rom 11:29)*

Principle 3

THE GREATER GOOD OF LEADERSHIP

1 Chronicles 21: 17

[17] And David said to God, "Was it not I who commanded the people to be numbered? I am the one who has sinned and done evil indeed; but these sheep, what have they done? Let Your hand, I pray, O Lord my God, be against me and my father's house, but not against Your people that they should be plagued."

I have seen an unusual injustice many times in corporate business settings and in positions of leadership where leaders and business owners are more than willing to quickly sacrifice their followers or employees in order to avoid taking responsibility for their own actions.

Well, you will be amazed to know – being a good leader means you take full responsibility for everything that happens under your authority.

The general argument that people make to justify their actions is that: (i) someone must be sacrificed for the greater good and (ii) if the head is brought down, everything else will be lost.

Truth is, if Christ had taken this approach, none of us would be walking in the glory of salvation today. Imagine Christ as the Good Shepherd adopting this philosophy – *"if I am out feeding the flock and a wolf comes by, I will just let it have one sheep and if it is eaten, well, it is eaten"*. Wisdom will say to you, if this is kept up, your flock of sheep will cease to exist, sooner or later.

In reality, it is the leader, rather than the followers, who ought to sacrifice the most and this is a principle that has been successfully used throughout the Bible. The greatest example of such excellent leadership principles is Jesus laying down His life for His sheep.

David, also in the above situation owned up to his sins instead of blaming it on the people. Therefore, it was no mere coincidence that David was so loved by his followers, so much so that they would have laid down their lives subsequently for him.

If you are still not convinced about the principle of a leader standing at the front at all times and taking full responsibility for failures occurring under his authority, whether by himself or others under him, then let me share these last two thoughts:

- You will achieve much more when your followers and workers have total confidence in you. This they will not do if you give them reason to believe that you will betray their trust rather than save and deliver them in times of difficulty.

- If you think it is best to sacrifice your followers in your place, you ought to understand that people are thinking beings. They understand that whatever happens to one of their kind is likely to happen to them too and if they have reason to think like this, you will find it almost impossible to deal with the eventual collusion and desertion by your your staff – after all, you are their common betrayer.

Always remember that the sheep are more than the shepherd and that they can cause a stampede when troubled.

Principle 4

CUSTOMER CARE V3.0

2 Chronicle 10: 6 – 11

6 Then King Rehoboam consulted the elders who stood before his father Solomon while he still lived, saying, "How do you advise me to answer these people?" 7 And they spoke to him, saying, "If you are kind to these people, and please them, and speak good words to them, they will be your servants forever." 8 But he rejected the advice which the elders had given him, and consulted the young men who had grown up with him, who stood before him. 9 And he said to them, "What advice do you give? How should we answer this people who have spoken to me, saying, 'Lighten the yoke which your father put on us'?" 10 Then the young men who had grown up with him spoke to him, saying, "Thus you should speak to the people who have spoken to you, saying, 'Your father made our yoke heavy, but you make it lighter on us'—thus you shall say to them: 'My little finger shall be thicker than my father's waist! 11 And now, whereas my father put a heavy yoke on you, I will add to your yoke; my father chastised you with whips, but I will chastise you with scourges!'"

This is what customer care is all about. I find it quite intriguing some leaders take the odd view that they don't run a shop so customer care does not apply to them – it applies to everyone in leadership position whether you own a shop or not.

Even politicians, who could easily argue they are not involved in any product selling to the general public, are not excluded because they actually sell ideology, expectations and political alternatives. So you see, as long as you are engaged with people, you are in the customer care business – except you have an entity or enterprise that functions successfully without any human involvement besides yourself.

On this occasion, I will allow myself to classify institutional and political leaders along with business persons all as one – business persons.

In order for your customers, clients or followers to be loyal to you over the long term, it takes three ingredients – deducing from the Biblical passage above:

1. ***Firstly, you need kindness - "be kind to them rather than harsh":*** Understand that they are coming to you because they chose you or your product over other available ones. That choice, more often than not, is based on the notion

that you will treat them better than the others may – treat them better in terms of your pricing, interactions – kindness in every facet of their engagement with you.

2. ***Secondly, please your customers – let their needs be your priority:*** It does not mean you need to do everything they ask of you. In fact, the original word for "*please them*" translates as "*be accepting of them*". In other words, listen to them. If you find good and innovative ways of listening to your customers or followers, they may even show you what services or products they prefer, as well as the next big thing they will be interested in.

The truth is, they know what they want, but are unable provide it for themselves which is why they come to you to meet their needs.

Business does not really have to be so difficult if you take great care to listen to your customers. Some organisations even conduct research to come up with new ideas for serving customers, but this same information could have been easily obtained by just talking to the customers. . More often than not, customers know exactly what it is they want and they might just tell you if you listen to them.

3. ***Finally, express your appreciation by speaking good words to them:*** Everybody likes to be appreciated. Customers and followers will tend to go where they feel they are treated better.

Very often this feeling is communicated through words. If you, as a leader, together with your staff staff develop the culture of speaking the right words of appreciation and gratitude in response to your customers' patronage, you will drastically increase your chances of getting their repeated patronage.

Words do matter, in fact, in the business of people, words matter the most, but it has to be done consciously, with sincerity and good intention.

Principle 5

FOLLOWING LEADS VRS INDIVIDUALITY

Ezra 10: 1 – 6

Now while Ezra was praying, and while he was confessing, weeping, and bowing down before the house of God, a very large assembly of men, women, and children gathered to him from Israel; for the people wept very bitterly. [2] And Shechaniah the son of Jehiel, one of the sons of Elam, spoke up and said to Ezra, "We have trespassed against our God, and have taken pagan wives from the peoples of the land; yet now there is hope in Israel in spite of this. [3] Now therefore, let us make a covenant with our God to put away all these wives and those who have been born to them, according to the advice of my master and of those who tremble at the commandment of our God; and let it be done according to the law. [4] Arise, for this matter is your responsibility. We also are with you. Be of good courage, and do it." [5] Then Ezra arose, and made the leaders of the priests, the Levites, and all Israel swear an oath that they would do according to this word. So they swore an oath. [6] Then Ezra rose up from before the house of God, and went into the chamber of

Jehohanan the son of Eliashib; and when he came there, he ate no bread and drank no water, for he mourned because of the guilt of those from the captivity.

The fact that you dwell in "the land" does not mean you ought to do what everybody in the land is doing.

The fact that everybody in the land the Israelites found themselves in was marrying pagan wives did not mean the children of Israel also had to because, unlike others, they were a peculiar people, a royal priesthood.

The fact that your business operates in a certain area, amongst a certain people, in a particular industry does not mean that you should do everything being done within those parameters.

As a leader, the fact that other leaders in your field are doing things in a certain way does not mean yours ought to do the same. Your uniqueness as a leader is not always defined by what you do. Most times, it is also defined by what you do not do.

Watch out! You may be doing or engaging a leadership style or business practice that everyone else is engaging in but which may be damaging your operations because of the uniqueness of your organisation's vision. It may actually be making you look dirty and filthy.

Remember, you are not just an ordinary leader or business person; you are a godly leader and business person.

Here is an analogy – the pig is already considered a dirty animal, so when it lies in filthy mud puddles, there is no contrary noticeable view about it – it is simply a dirty animal, lying in dirt. On the contrary, if you get a beautiful white cat to jump into the same mud, the contrasting view of a "dirty cat" becomes apparent very quickly.

Principle 6

DELEGATING WITH BACKING AUTHORITY

Nehemiah 2: 4 – 9

4 Then the king said to me, "What do you request?" So I prayed to the God of heaven. 5 And I said to the king, "If it pleases the king, and if your servant has found favour in your sight, I ask that you send me to Judah, to the city of my fathers' tombs, that I may rebuild it." 6 Then the king said to me (the queen also sitting beside him), "How long will your journey be? And when will you return?" So it pleased the king to send me; and I set him a time. 7 Furthermore I said to the king, "If it pleases the king, let letters be given to me for the governors of the region beyond the River,[a] that they must permit me to pass through till I come to Judah, 8 and a letter to Asaph the keeper of the king's forest, that he must give me timber to make beams for the gates of the citadel which pertains to the temple,[b] for the city wall, and for the house that I will occupy." And the king granted them to me according to the good hand of my God upon me. 9 Then I went to the governors in the region beyond the River, and gave them the king's letters. Now the king had sent captains of the army and horsemen with me.

❧❧ ❧❧ ❧❧

Authority delegated must also be clearly communicated to the persons who are to be subjected to it.

One should not be done without the other. If authority has been delegated and this information is not communicated to those who fall under it, then that authority will soon become useless in the hands of the one to whom it was delegated. This is a principle that works in business, the church or even in the home.

Nehemiah understood the principle – hence his request of the king to write to all stakeholders he was likely to come across on the journey back to Jerusalem. This was an important dissemination to back the King's authority given him to go back and rebuild the temple of the Lord.

When a specific authority has been known to be associated with certain persons and it is now to be exercised by someone else, then the original bearer of such authority must of necessity communicate the transfer of such authority so as to alter the perceived association between him and such authority.

The communication process acts as a means of informing all stakeholders that the authority in question was willingly released and received. In the absence of that overt exhibition of the transfer, any new bearer of this authority will be considered as using it illegitimately or going against the unilateral respect for that authority. The result is usually a tendency for employees or followers to collectively undermine or disrespect the new bearer of such authority. Once such a notion is associated with the new bearer of the authority, the damage can go even further because, more often than not, it lingers on even after the transfer is subsequently ratified.

It is a common mistake made in business and on many leadership platforms. Delegating or transferring authority without communicating it to the core stakeholders of that authority not only destroys the good standing of the new leader – it also weakens the effectiveness of the authority he has been delegated.

Principle 7

TESTING IDEAS AND VISIONS BEFORE USE

Nehemiah 2: 11 – 18

11 So I came to Jerusalem and was there three days. 12 Then
I arose in the night, I and a few men with me; I told no one
what my God had put in my heart to do at Jerusalem; nor
was there any animal with me, except the one on which I
rode. 13 And I went out by night through the Valley Gate to
the Serpent Well and the Refuse Gate, and viewed the walls
of Jerusalem which were broken down and its gates which
were burned with fire. 14 Then I went on to the Fountain
Gate and to the King's Pool, but there was no room for the
animal under me to pass. 15 So I went up in the night by the
valley, and viewed the wall; then I turned back and entered
by the Valley Gate, and so returned. 16 And the officials did
not know where I had gone or what I had done; I had not
yet told the Jews, the priests, the nobles, the officials, or the
others who did the work. 17 Then I said to them, "You see the
distress that we are in, how Jerusalem lays waste, and its
gates are burned with fire. Come and let us build the wall
of Jerusalem, that we may no longer be a reproach." 18 And I

told them of the hand of my God which had been good upon me, and also of the king's words that he had spoken to me. So they said, "Let us rise up and build." Then they set their hands to this good work.

As a leader, it is in your heart God most certainly puts ideas and visions about the future destiny of the business, home, church or organisation you are leading.

But be reminded, in your eagerness to succeed, there is the tendency to hastily run off and end up listening to the devil instead of God. The first step, when you believe you have received guidance as to what to do is not to disclose anything to those you are leading, even if you strongly feel it is God speaking to you. Test the vision first, through these six levels Nehemiah exemplifies from verse 13 onwards:

Go out at night – this means, first consider the idea or vision in total quietness, when others are asleep and you are separated from the noisy doubts and pessimism of the people around you. It ensures that your atmosphere of thinking and spiritual engagement with the vision or idea (as its first recipient) is devoid of all unnecessary physical, emotional and religious noises of distraction.

Run the idea through the Valley gate – the valley is conceivably the lowest part enclosed by two hills or mountains. Consider thoroughly whether continuing with this idea and its outcomes is likely to bring your organisation or the beneficiaries of the idea or vision to a low point and leave it there, or if it has the ability to raise the organisation and the people to the top of the mountain too – i.e. the peak of fulfilment on an individual and corporate level.

Bring the idea, vision or plan to the Serpent Well – a well, naturally, is meant to give us water- living water from the word of God, not serpents. This is a test to see whether the idea, vision or plan is in line with the law or word of God or the law of the world or satan *(serpent well).*

Stop and let this plan, idea or vision be run past the Refuse Gate. Sin is what makes us stink like the refuse dump; This section tests your vision or idea, to see if there is any part of it – at the beginning, middle or end, that would bring about the commission of sin of any kind *(and there is no small or big sin, there's only sin).* If so, then you ought to think again about it.

Follow through to the Fountain Gate – this, traditionally, is the gate that leads into an open court fountain where temple goers wash (refresh) their feet and faces before entering the synagogue. It is a test of whether or not the vision or idea is capable of refreshing its beneficiaries, organisation or your business. Will it have a positive or negative impact?

Finally, does the plan or vision have the potential to bring you into the Kings Court – in other words, does it have the ability to put you at the very top, set you above and apart and establish you as a king or pioneer. History is written about kings and nobles and not about ordinary men. History is about achievers and pioneers, not average folks. Hence, if it is God's plan or idea in your heart, it should also possess the ability to bring you into a position of being a pacesetter.

With all these tests, you can determine if the matter was one put in your heart by God. Only after having your idea pass through all these gates should you then communicate it to your employees, followers, customers or stakeholders.

Principle 8

EFFICIENCY THROUGH HUMAN CAPITAL AUDITS

Number 1: 1 – 5

Now the Lord spoke to Moses in the Wilderness of Sinai, in the tabernacle of meeting, on the first day of the second month, in the second year after they had come out of the land of Egypt, saying: [2] "Take a census of all the congregation of the children of Israel, by their families, by their fathers' houses, according to the number of names, every male individually, [3] from twenty years old and above—all who are able to go to war in Israel. You and Aaron shall number them by their armies. [4] And with you there shall be a man from every tribe, each one the head of his father's house. [5] "These are the names of the men who shall stand with you: from Reuben, Elizur the son of Shedeur.

This passage exemplifies a strategic activity many leaders and businesses people do not readily do, or if done at all, gets done when something goes wrong or when the organisation is forced to consider it.

The whole idea of the census in this Bible passage involving Moses and Aaron as senior executives was not merely for the purpose of assessing the number of Israelites. In Biblical days, every tribe had specific duties assigned to them, including those of a social, religious and military nature.

Figuratively, the passage teaches that leaders and business people need to regularly engage in auditing their human resources' knowledge and skills stock.

Once your organisation or business has worked out what combination of skills, expertise and other human resource activities make it successful, these should be maintained by conducting regular audits to find out where there are shortfalls and the need for replacements or upgrades. This is a sure means of maintaining your success.

As in the passage above, this kind of human resource auditing is even more crucial when an organisation or business is about to make medium to long term changes in any aspect of its operations. It requires that you consider very thoroughly the new direction and goals of the organisation and the human resources needed to move the institution from its current position to the intended new heights.

You would then be able to tell what new human capital is needed, which of the current ones need to be disposed of and those that can and should be upgraded.

Disposing of resources is usually a hard leadership

-cum-business decision, but in extreme circumstances, you might actually need to downsize. Hard as it may be, letting people go from time to time may conflict with your sympathetic nature as a human, but remember, God's vision, in which you have been employed a leader is far more important.

Principle 9

HANDLING THE SPREAD OF PROBLEMS

Numbers 5: 1 – 4

And the Lord spoke to Moses, saying: [2] "Command the children of Israel that they put out of the camp every leper, everyone who has a discharge, and whoever becomes defiled by a corpse. [3] You shall put out both male and female; you shall put them outside the camp, that they may not defile their camps in the midst of which I dwell." [4] And the children of Israel did so, and put them outside the camp; as the Lord spoke to Moses, so the children of Israel did.

As a leader or business manager there will come times that hard and harsh decisions will have to be made. In the passage above, the Bible portrays the need to isolate some components of the organisation or business in order to save the greater part.

The word *"discharge"* in the passage can be used to apply to any internal component that has the likelihood of jeopardizing the overall success of any organization or business. For the purposes of this book, "*component*" may refer to a product, a policy, a concept, a strategy, a person, a division or a branch of the organisation, business or political party.

The important learning point here for leadership application is that as soon as the state of a component is assessed as likely to contaminate the greater entity, it has to be immediately isolated and repaired for possible re-integration.

For example, an employee or follower can be considered as defiling *(contaminating)* the rest of the business or organisation by say, "*discharges*" of unhealthy attitude, counter-productivity, rumour mongering, disregard for authority or breeding dissent. Such a person and others that have been badly defiled by associating will need to be isolated before the entire entity gets contaminated.

The example could also be applied to a business product within the organisation that has a *discharge* of bad customer reviews or bad publicity. This product would need to be immediately isolated and dealt with before it destroys the good reviews and saleability of the other products.

How long isolation takes is a decision that needs to be based purely on:

(i) the damage caused so far,

(ii) the likelihood of further damage that can be caused if re-integration is permitted

(iii) the cost of re-integration. Especially in cases where the component to be isolated is influential or significant within the entity

Some amount of creative thinking needs to go into structuring how the isolation can be carried out without having a negative overall impact.

Principle 10

SPREADING THE VISION = SPREADING THE BURDEN

Numbers 11: 10 – 17

*10 Then Moses heard the people weeping throughout their
families, everyone at the door of his tent; and the anger of
the Lord was greatly aroused; Moses also was displeased.
11 So Moses said to the Lord, "Why have You afflicted Your
servant? And why have I not found favour in Your sight,
that You have laid the burden of all these people on me?
12 Did I conceive all these people? Did I beget them, that You
should say to me, 'Carry them in your bosom, as a guard-
ian carries a nursing child,' to the land which You swore
to their fathers? 13 Where am I to get meat to give to all
these people? For they weep all over me, saying, 'Give us
meat, that we may eat.' 14 I am not able to bear all these
people alone, because the burden is too heavy for me. 15 If
You treat me like this, please kill me here and now—if I
have found favour in Your sight—and do not let me see my
wretchedness!" 16 So the Lord said to Moses: "Gather to Me
seventy men of the elders of Israel, whom you know to be
the elders of the people and officers over them; bring them*

to the tabernacle of meeting, that they may stand there with you. [17] *Then I will come down and talk with you there. I will take of the Spirit that is upon you and will put the same upon them; and they shall bear the burden of the people with you, that you may not bear it yourself alone.*

As a business owner or visionary or the most senior person in an organisation it is often quite easy to want to do everything yourself.

You may have employed deputies or other workers to help you, but you are still carrying the burden all by yourself. In the biblical context above, Moses already knew the elders were meant to help him, but he was not receiving the full benefit of their help because of a principle he was failing to apply and which Jehovah had to show him unambiguously.

Until now, Moses, was the only man receiving face to face visions from God. Everybody else's knowledge of the grand vision came only from the bits and pieces that Moses spoke to them or the commands he gave. This was miniscule, compared to the detailed plans Moses had been receiving from God.

Finally, God had to get Moses to come up to the mountain with the elders and there He cast the grand vision before them all. Suddenly the elders saw a clearer picture of where Israel was supposed to be headed.

It was now possible for the elders to make informed assessments of how to fulfil the vision, how their own strengths and weaknesses fitted in and the kind of help they could give to Moses in getting all of Israel there. Until Moses brought the elders to the same level of his understanding of the grand vision, he never received any proper help from them. He bore the burden alone.

The lesson to learn is this: In your position as a leader or business person manning an organisation big enough to require help and support, consciously allow the people helping you see the big picture and where exactly they each fit

into it. It helps them better assess what they possess that can be useful for the journey and it also makes them a part of the journey, not passengers who may be kicked off along the way.

Leaders and business owners need to SHARE the vision in the clearest way possible, so that your immediate helpers can begin to own the vision as theirs since people tend to work better for a vision owned, than for one borrowed.

Interestingly, seventy elders were chosen by God. The number seven in Hebrew is *"Ayin"*, representing *"an eye"* or better still, translated as *"to know"*.

In other words, it was not really about seventy old men going to the top of a mountain, rather it was a way devised by God to teach Moses that in order for him to progress much more efficiently in leadership and the management of Israel, his executives NEED to see and know the vision in exactly the same way God had made Moses understand it.

Thus we learn that the vision driving the workers must not be different from the vision held by their leader.

Principle 11

NEGOTIATION AND PERSUASIVE COMMUNICATION

Numbers 14: 11 - 21

11 Then the Lord said to Moses: "How long will these people reject Me? And how long will they not believe Me, with all the signs which I have performed among them? 12 I will strike them with the pestilence and disinherit them, and I will make of you a nation greater and mightier than they."
13 And Moses said to the Lord: "Then the Egyptians will hear it, for by Your might You brought these people up from among them, 14 and they will tell it to the inhabitants of this land. They have heard that You, Lord, are among these people; that You, Lord, are seen face to face and Your cloud stands above them, and You go before them in a pillar of cloud by day and in a pillar of fire by night. 15 Now if You kill these people as one man, then the nations which have heard of Your fame will speak, saying, 16 'Because the Lord was not able to bring this people to the land which He swore to give them, therefore He killed them in the wilderness.'
17 And now, I pray, let the power of my Lord be great, just as You have spoken, saying, 18 'The Lord is longsuffering and

abundant in mercy, forgiving iniquity and transgression; but He by no means clears the guilty, visiting the iniquity of the fathers on the children to the third and fourth generation.' [19] *Pardon the iniquity of this people, I pray, according to the greatness of Your mercy, just as You have forgiven this people, from Egypt even until now."* [20] *Then the Lord said: "I have pardoned, according to your word;* [21] *but truly, as I live, all the earth shall be filled with the glory of the Lord."*

Negotiation takes many forms and indeed a huge amount of investigation and preparations go into it.

I am certain there are many books out there on negotiation and persuasiveness but here, in the text above, Moses faces the huge task of having to persuade no other person but God Almighty, not to take a certain course of action – wiping out Israel.

Moses does not particularly give a structured approach, but crucially, he teaches *"pressure points"* to apply in convincing anyone to either take or change a course of action.

Pressure Point 1 (verse 13-14): From God, the highest, to the lowest petty thief, everyone has some reputation to uphold. How certain special people perceive our reputation matters to us more than how everybody else sees it. For these special people, our reputation is very likely the only credible currency we can deal with them in – as such, how well or bad they see our reputation means a lot to us.

In the case of God, His reputation in the eyes of the Egyptians would have been ruined if His intended action had gone ahead and come to the knowledge of the Egyptians; because He delivered Israel from destruction at the hands of Egypt - the very act He now wanted to carry out against them.

So, the pressure point is: point out the action intended is one they had previously discredited. You should emphasize the possibility of their action(s) becoming known to the person or organisation they previously discredited for taking the same action and how it can be lethally used by the latter.

To discredit a thing and subsequently credit it makes any leader or organisation appear to lack firmness.

Pressure Point 2 (verse 14a): Make it clear to the party that any blot on their reputation is likely to spread beyond just those who know them. In verse 14 of the passage, Moses warns God that the blot on His reputation was not only going to be known in Egypt– it would spread much further abroad. For a business leader, the spread of a negative reputation can lead not only to the loss of existing customers and followers, but also of potential ones. The possible magnitude of such an outcome is enough to make anyone re-think their decision.

Pressure Point 3 (verse 14b): A third pressure point to affect any party's decision on a given matter is to consider whether or not their intended action will dilute, taint or flaw the magnitude of the person's previous achievements.

In verse 14b, Moses recounts to God the great things that He had done for Israel in the past and which many had heard about. Indirectly, Moses was asking the question *"do You want all these glorious past acts to be tainted by this one act that You are about to engage in?"*

Pressure Point 4 (Verse 15): Nobody likes to have anything to do with a leader who exercises no discretion.

It portrays a person about whom no one is sure whether he will deal with people on a merited basis or indiscriminately deal with everybody in the same manner. Here in this verse, Moses is asking God, *"don't you think You may appear as unstable if You should wipe out over three million Israelites as though they were just one man?"* And therein lies the fourth pressure point – will the intended action paint a picture of an individual who is unstable and deals with people indiscriminately?

Pressure Point 5 (verse 16): Another pressure point to consider is whether an intended action will expose an actual or perceived inefficiency or incompetence on the part of the leader. The truth is, every leader likes to be seen as highly competent and people are likely to weigh their perceptions very carefully if the actions of the leader appear incompetent.

Pressure Point 6 (verses 17-18): Finally, a tie-breaker pressure point to consider is this – look out for any previous actions, utterances and engagements of the person you are trying to convince that is opposite to their intended actions but parallel to the course of action you want them to take. When you do find it, encourage him to consider taking those same actions.

If such pressure points of persuasion worked with God, it will certainly work with humans.

Principle 12

THE "WHERE" OF SOCIAL RESPONSIBILITY

Numbers 36: 1 – 9

Now the chief fathers of the families of the children of Gilead the son of Machir, the son of Manasseh, of the families of the sons of Joseph, came near and spoke before Moses and before the leaders, the chief fathers of the children of Israel. [2] And they said: "The Lord commanded my lord Moses to give the land as an inheritance by lot to the children of Israel, and my lord was commanded by the Lord to give the inheritance of our brother Zelophehad to his daughters. [3] Now if they are married to any of the sons of the other tribes of the children of Israel, then their inheritance will be taken from the inheritance of our fathers, and it will be added to the inheritance of the tribe into which they marry; so it will be taken from the lot of our inheritance. [4] And when the Jubilee of the children of Israel comes, then their inheritance will be added to the inheritance of the tribe into which they marry; so their inheritance will be taken away from the inheritance of the tribe of our fathers." [5] Then Moses commanded the children of Israel according to the word of the

Lord, saying: "What the tribe of the sons of Joseph speaks
is right. [6] *This is what the Lord commands concerning the*
daughters of Zelophehad, saying, 'Let them marry whom
they think best, but they may marry only within the family
of their father's tribe.' [7] *So the inheritance of the children of*
Israel shall not change hands from tribe to tribe, for every
one of the children of Israel shall keep the inheritance of
the tribe of his fathers. [8] *And every daughter who possesses*
an inheritance in any tribe of the children of Israel shall be
the wife of one of the family of her father's tribe, so that the
children of Israel each may possess the inheritance of his
fathers. [9] *Thus no inheritance shall change hands from one*
tribe to another, but every tribe of the children of Israel shall
keep its own inheritance."

What I am about to say may not sound right at all in the secular world of business. It will certainly NOT sit well with the way the world has taught us to lead or conduct business.

But of course it should not be – and if you are reading this book, you most certainly want to do business or run your organisation "the God way".

The tribe you come from must always benefit from the success *(inheritances)* of your business or leadership.

It does not matter where your business or leadership is operating globally, or where you or your clients are based. By all means, do business *(or lead)* throughout the world, but let the final benefits or legacies of such a leadership or business enterprise be reflected in the tribe you come from. Your tribe primarily refers to your country of origin and the family from which you came. This could be the family into which you were born as well as your spiritual family that nurtured your spirit man.

It is a divine principle. God created you as a leader in a particular country, family and church. Therefore, if He had wanted the benefits and legacies of your leadership or business success to belong to a *"tribe"* other than that from which you were hewn, He would have placed you into another family or country. Think about it.

With the same level therefore that organisations honour their immediate "social responsibilities," I often recommend that these acts must find a means to extend beyond the immediate town or country where the entity is located and cover the areas from which its founder(s) hail from, assuming they are different

Principle 13

EFFECTIVE COMMUNICATIONS THROUGH VISUALIZATION

Exodus 4: 1 – 7

Then Moses answered and said, "But suppose they will not believe me or listen to my voice; suppose they say, 'The Lord has not appeared to you.'" [2] So the Lord said to him, "What is that in your hand?" He said, "A rod." [3] And He said, "Cast it on the ground." So he cast it on the ground, and it became a serpent; and Moses fled from it. [4] Then the Lord said to Moses, "Reach out your hand and take it by the tail" (and he reached out his hand and caught it, and it became a rod in his hand), [5] "that they may believe that the Lord God of their fathers, the God of Abraham, the God of Isaac, and the God of Jacob, has appeared to you." [6] Furthermore the Lord said to him, "Now put your hand in your bosom." And he put his hand in his bosom, and when he took it out, behold, his hand was leprous, like snow. [7] And He said, "Put your hand in your bosom again." So he put his hand in his bosom again, and drew it out of his bosom, and behold, it was restored like his other flesh.

❦ ❦ ❦

Here is Moses before God. He has been given a word to speak in order for Israel to identify with him as their leader. Moses questions God – "what if Israel does NOT hear the special password you gave me?"

Many people mistake Moses as merely complaining - truth is he was not. He understood a fundamental principle in leadership and running - what you see makes a more lasting impact on you than what you hear.

Psychologically, what you see is immediately impressed on your mind, whereas what you hear, less so because it has to go through the process of being transformed from words into images before it is registered. Even then, the final image might be distorted during the process.

The same principle is very well established in marketing and sales. – it is much easier to make an impact on a customer by letting them see your product in action than to hear you talk about its amazing properties.

A picture speaks volumes than many words can. The visible miracles that Moses performed before Israel were certainly more effective in convincing them that he was sent by their God. No amount of words would have brought about the result he got. In managing people, leadership by example takes its root from here – they see you do it.

If you can demonstrate visually what you expect from your employees, you are more likely to win them over to follow your ideals and principles. Take the business of the home, for example. Children are easily moulded by what they see parents do, not by long speeches.

It is also much easier to persuade business associates, customers, partners, employees if they can see what you are saying. In cases where you cannot realistically provide people with a visual aid or a tool such as a video, make sure that the description of what you need them to understand is vivid enough to capture their imagination.

People tend to be drawn to what makes a vivid impression on their minds as it ignites the inner energy that makes them want to follow a vision or purchase a product. On the other hand, if all you paint is a dull picture of gloom and hard work, there would really be little reason to follow such a vision.

As it is written in *Proverbs 27:20*, *"the eyes are never full"*. It is a mystery you can use to your advantage. The next time you try explaining something to someone, try making them SEE what you want to SAY.

Principle 14

HOW TO MANAGE ORGANISATIONAL CHANGE

Exodus 13:17-22

Then it came to pass, when Pharaoh had let the people go, that God did not lead them by way of the land of the Philistines, although that was near; for God said, "Lest perhaps the people change their minds when they see war, and return to Egypt." 18 *So God led the people around by way of the wilderness of the Red Sea. And the children of Israel went up in orderly ranks out of the land of Egypt.* 19 *And Moses took the bones of Joseph with him, for he had placed the children of Israel under solemn oath, saying, "God will surely visit you, and you shall carry up my bones from here with you."* 20 *So they took their journey from Succoth and camped in Etham at the edge of the wilderness.* 21 *And the Lord went before them by day in a pillar of cloud to lead the way, and by night in a pillar of fire to give them light, so as to go by day and night.* 22 *He did not take away the pillar of cloud by day or the pillar of fire by night from before the people.*

The way God deals with Israel after taking them out of Egypt presents a phenomenal lesson on how to manage organisational change the God way.

Every organisation will at some point need to engage in some form of change, whether it is a change in the way customers are treated or how production is done or how relationships in the organisation are managed. Now change, irrespective of its size or setting will only succeed if everybody gets behind it.

The truth however, is that by nature, humans resist change. God realized that Israel had over the years become used to slavery and no longer saw themselves as the warriors they were blessed to be. He, therefore, had to find a way to ensure that in the early stages of Israel's change process *(moving from Egypt to Canaan)*, they were NOT exposed to any condition or situation that would make them consider Egypt was a better option. In other words, God did not immediately expose them to wars in case it caused them to immediately retract back to their new default mentality of "being slaves."

From this we learn it is essential when leading a change process, to first identify the likely challenges along the way which could tempt the organisation back into the former status-quo.

One strategy for managing change is to make sure that at all times during the process, the ONLY viable option made available to the organisation is *option of "change" (not the Egypt they left behind).* No other option should be presented that may remotely motivate them to choose the old way.

Notice that God had to also adapt His leadership style during this transition process. If you read from verses 21-22, He led them by day in a cloud to provide shade from the sun and by night as a fire to provide light. This means that in times of change, the leader should take a proactive role in ensuring that he leads the organisation from the *"front"* during the *"day."*

During the day the people already have light, motivation, enthusiasm, the drive and all that is needed to work towards the set destination. This is the change season in which the leader takes a forefront position to give directions and to channel all their energies and motivation into the appropriate focal purpose.

Like a pillar of cloud *(whirlwinds)*, he needs to rise above those he is leading in order to see ahead of the people, clearing any obstruction in his path. This approach to management recognizes that in the day time when all things seem to be working well, much ground will be covered before the darkness comes.

The night time is the period when motivation is down, when the employees or followers cannot see clearly and when the energy levels are low - it is when the leader should lead from behind.

Leading from behind as a pillar of fire ensures that light is made available on the path of the marching organisation. It means, for the leader to be the guiding light in the dark, he possesses enough knowledge of the change process that the rest of the entity can rely on.

The fire by night also takes away the cold (or provides warmth) – meaning, the leader should endeavour to completely remove demoralising factors and produce energy among the people.

Acting as a fire behind the people, also ensures that no fears, doubts, discouragements, turbulences and distractions sneak in, from behind the people to reverse the many miles of progress they may have gained during the day. This is a leader's focus during the night.

This is a basic overview of critical considerations to make during change management.

Principle 15

DEALING WITH DIFFICULT SITUATIONS

Exodus 14: 10 – 18

10 And when Pharaoh drew near, the children of Israel lifted their eyes, and behold, the Egyptians marched after them. So they were very afraid, and the children of Israel cried out to the Lord. 11 Then they said to Moses, "Because there were no graves in Egypt, have you taken us away to die in the wilderness? Why have you so dealt with us, to bring us up out of Egypt? 12 Is this not the word that we told you in Egypt, saying, 'Let us alone that we may serve the Egyptians'? For it would have been better for us to serve the Egyptians than that we should die in the wilderness." 13 And Moses said to the people, "Do not be afraid. Stand still, and see the salvation of the Lord, which He will accomplish for you today. For the Egyptians whom you see today, you shall see again no more forever. 14 The Lord will fight for you, and you shall hold your peace." 15 And the Lord said to Moses, "Why do you cry to Me? Tell the children of Israel to go forward. 16 But lift up your rod, and stretch out your hand over the sea and divide it. And the children of Israel shall go on dry ground through the midst of the sea. [17] And I indeed will harden the hearts of the Egyptians, and they shall follow them. So I will gain honour over Pharaoh and over all his army, his chariots, and his horsemen. [18] Then the Egyptians shall know that I am the Lord, when I have gained honour for Myself over Pharaoh, his chariots, and his horsemen."

Every leader, business or political organisation in its lifetime will experience difficulty. It is a natural and spiritual part of man's existence, and how this is handled as an individual is different from how it is handled when you are leading others.

Here, Moses displays a very fundamental three step process in dealing with hard times:

1. ***Firstly, he ignores the whining of some of the followers*** – There will always be people during the hard times who will describe the reason everything is going wrong and how they had "*told you so*" in the past. Moses did not banish them because he understood that he would need them in the future, so he simply ignores them. He makes a conscious choice not to be distracted by their whining.

2. ***Secondly, he does the most significant thing in the entire problem management process*** – he calms their fears and stabilizes the situation.

Notice that Moses at this point did not really know what the next step was going to be, but he realized that if he did not allay their fears, things would get worse. He understood that if he allowed the people to continue in fear, this will only force them to make decisions driven by negative emotions which would only complicate matters.

In managing any situation, the first and most immediate step should be to stabilize it whilst you seek a lasting solution. For businesses, this stabilisation process will not only apply to your staff, but also to clients and other stakeholders with whom you have to deal.

In the above passage, Moses shows us a good way to carry out such stabilization – *by making it clear that the situation was only temporary*. This brings back confidence and hope as well as provides assurance that whatever the present circumstances, things will return to normal soon, even as Moses told them: "*...the Egyptians you **see** today, you shall see them **no more**.*"

3. ***After he succeeded in stabilising the situation, he then lifts up his hands and rod simultaneously.*** His hands represent prayer, while the rod his skill, authority, favour, insight and power to work.

   Therefore, he raises both in order to find LASTING solutions. Like Moses, a leader's objective is to, if possible; totally prevent such a problem from ever recurring. This was why Pharaoh's whole army had to drown.

   Moses didn't just pray and sit down to wait on God's action – he also took action. Lasting solutions will always be collaborations between God and man on earth.

Principle 16

EFFECTIVE SUCCESSION PLANNING FOR CONTINUITY

Exodus 17: 8 – 16

8 *Now Amalek came and fought with Israel in Rephidim.*
9 *And Moses said to Joshua, "Choose us some men and go*
out, fight with Amalek. Tomorrow I will stand on the top
of the hill with the rod of God in my hand." 10 *So Joshua*
did as Moses said to him, and fought with Amalek. And
Moses, Aaron, and Hur went up to the top of the hill.
11 *And so it was, when Moses held up his hand, that Israel*
prevailed; and when he let down his hand, Amalek pre-
vailed. 12 *But Moses' hands became heavy; so they took a*
stone and put it under him, and he sat on it. And Aaron
and Hur supported his hands, one on one side, and the
other on the other side; and his hands were steady until
the going down of the sun. 13 *So Joshua defeated Amalek*
and his people with the edge of the sword. 14 *Then the*
Lord said to Moses, "Write this for a memorial in the
book and recount it in the hearing of Joshua, that I will
utterly blot out the remembrance of Amalek from under
heaven." 15 *And Moses built an altar and called its name,*

The-Lord-Is-My-Banner [16] *for he said, "Because the Lord has sworn: the Lord will have war with Amalek from generation to generation."*

Many organisations fail after the founding visionaries die and it is not difficult to see why. It is because they had done no succession planning.

In the very early stages after the Red Sea experience, Moses has already started training Joshua and others for succession, specifying quite clearly, exactly how it should be done.

Moses envisages the nation of Israel continuing after his departure, so he starts to make provision for others to succeed him.

Until one sees a business, organisation, institution, government or family as continuing beyond their existence, it will be hard to see the need preparing anyone to carry on after we are gone. Until we recognize that it is not us but God who determines our end, we will not see the need to start our succession planning NOW.

Most leaders may want to wait till they are *"close to the end"* before starting such planning, when in fact they may never know the *"end"* and even if they did get to it, never have the same energy to groom a successor properly.

So just how should you go about succession planning?

Moses tells Joshua to manage the war with Amalek. Carefully notice the stages in this activity as Moses allows Joshua to experience the ENTIRE process of one war from the beginning to the end, just like you should do with a prospective successor in your business or organization.

This is what Joshua is allowed to do:

(i) *Plan the war* – thus developing his visionary foresight
(ii) *Select the army* – practice how to source, allocate and manage resources
(iii) *Lead the soldiers into battle* – practicing real-time leadership in developing strategy, positioning, delegation, dealing with the complaints and fears of his soldiers etc.
(iv) *Defeat the enemy: completing the task and producing the desired result* – Moses, on the other hand, stayed AWAY from Joshua's fight BUT his rod and hands were raised in prayer - meaning Moses threw all his support behind Joshua.

Several other wars would have been fought like this, but the most important thing Moses was doing here was to establish a winning spirit in Joshua so he would start to believe more in his own abilities. He needed to believe that winning was possible even if Moses was not directly involved in the process.

It is no surprise, therefore, that later in scripture, when the soldiers were sent to spy out the land of Canaan, Joshua and Caleb were the only ones who believed the land could be conquered. Joshua had been taught to know nothing other than winning.

It is also obvious that when Moses died and someone had to take over, the mantle would logically fall to Joshua. This was no coincidence since Moses had started the process of grooming for quite some time prior to the need to replace him as leader had arisen.

This is the ideal approach to succession planning, in that prospective leaders are trained in the needed skills ahead of time with enough time for real-time display of nurtured skills.

Principle 17

VISION CASTING, DELEGATION AND GOVERNANCE

Exodus 18: 13 – 23

13 And so it was, on the next day, that Moses sat to judge
the people; and the people stood before Moses from morn-
ing until evening. 14 So when Moses' father-in-law saw all
that he did for the people, he said, "What is this thing that
you are doing for the people? Why do you alone sit, and all
the people stand before you from morning until evening?"
15 And Moses said to his father-in-law, "Because the people
come to me to inquire of God. 16 When they have a difficulty,
they come to me, and I judge between one and another;
and I make known the statutes of God and His laws." 17 So
Moses' father-in-law said to him, "The thing that you do is
not good. 18 Both you and these people who are with you
will surely wear yourselves out. For this thing is too much
for you; you are not able to perform it by yourself. 19 Listen
now to my voice; I will give you counsel, and God will be
with you: Stand before God for the people, so that you may
bring the difficulties to God. 20 And you shall teach them the
statutes and the laws, and show them the way in which they

must walk and the work they must do. [21] Moreover you shall select from all the people able men, such as fear God, men of truth, hating covetousness; and place such over them to be rulers of thousands, rulers of hundreds, rulers of fifties, and rulers of tens. [22] And let them judge the people at all times. Then it will be that every great matter they shall bring to you, but every small matter they themselves shall judge. So it will be easier for you, for they will bear the burden with you. [23] If you do this thing, and God so commands you, then you will be able to endure, and all this people will also go to their place in peace."

Here is Moses' father-in-law teaching him how to literally set up a governance system. Every country, business or institution requires a system within which to operate.

Jethro brought this understanding to Moses – that proper delegation of duties is one of the key factors in running an effective organisation. Delegating responsibility allows the leader time to deal with bigger picture issues.

Jethro was a priest and with Moses receiving priestly training from him whilst in exile, the latter also became a priest in his own right. Jethro was not just Moses' father-in-law, he was also his mentor, and a good one too. Mind you, Jethro had seven daughters, meaning that he was operating under the anointing of the seven Spirits of God, making him a very complete priest, advisor and mentor.

The point to be learnt from the above passage is that although Moses had effectively now graduated from being a shepherd under Jethro to now a priest and ruler of Israel, he kept his mentor close by. Such an act saved his destiny and that of Israel.

If Jethro's advice had not come in due time, he would have died from the pressure of leading Israel. The result, most likely would have been that Israel wouldn't have made it to the Promised Land or worse - they would have returned to Egypt.

As a leader, it is essential to understand that becoming mature, proficient, or advanced in your skills and abilities does not warrant discarding your mentors.

I say this to all business persons, leaders of organisations and married couples: "The day you cease to have a mentor, the people you are leading cease to be safe." Every leader must of a necessity have someone or a core group of persons they still look up to. If you choose not to have a mentor or someone to look up to or seek advice from, you have effectively ruled out yourself from being someone anybody else should look up to – and that is not the safest position for any wise leader to be in.

Here is an interesting point to note – Moses never sent for Jethro in the passage above. The latter, as a good mentor, was always looking out for Moses. We never hear of Jethro visiting Moses since he departed until now, because he understood his place in the scheme of Moses' destiny as a leader of Israel. He had no business interfering or being excessively inquisitive about Moses' affairs; nevertheless, he kept an eye and ear open for Moses and only came into the picture when he considered it to be absolutely necessary.

Jesus, in all His fullness and completeness, still remarks in *John 5:30 – "I can of Myself do nothing. As I hear, I judge; and My judgment is righteous, because I do not seek My own will but the will of the Father who sent Me".*

Think about it – no leader has it all. And this is the greatest test in determining which leader will soon fall and the one who will remain standing. The leader that says, "I need no one to look up to", has just made himself God and has already fallen – he just doesn't know it yet.

It really is not enough for anyone to simply say "I look up to God" – God is in Heaven above and we all look up to Him, but He has established men here on earth to represent Him. The Centurion says it differently in *Mathew 8: 9 – "For I also am a man under authority, having soldiers under me..."* signifying that a man cannot be in authority if he himself is not under authority.

Principle 18

LOYALTY VRS ALLEGIANCES

Exodus 32: 25 – 29

[25] Now when Moses saw that the people were unrestrained (for Aaron had not restrained them, to their shame among their enemies), [26] then Moses stood in the entrance of the camp, and said, "Whoever is on the Lord's side—come to me!" And all the sons of Levi gathered themselves together to him. [27] And he said to them, "Thus says the Lord God of Israel: 'Let every man put his sword on his side, and go in and out from entrance to entrance throughout the camp, and let every man kill his brother, every man his companion, and every man his neighbour.'" [28] So the sons of Levi did according to the word of Moses. And about three thousand men of the people fell that day. [29] Then Moses said, "Consecrate yourselves today to the Lord, that He may bestow on you a blessing this day, for every man has opposed his son and his brother."

For every leader of an organisation, especially political and business, there will be two big things on which eternal success is hinged.

The first is the vision or the bigger picture. In the above scriptural context, this is represented by Israel following God – Elohim is their vision.

The second is total commitment to following the bigger picture. This is because no matter how good a leader is, he is not always going to be with the people every day, even as it was with Moses. Sometimes the leader has to go away to do what only he can do, and this becomes a time when the loyalty of the employees or followers will be tested.

Here Moses shows the hard stand that a leader ought to take in such circumstances. Firstly, there is the understanding that nobody is above the bigger vision of the organisation, not even the leader or chief executive, Moses.

Without mincing words, Moses made a call for those that still stood by the vision and believed in it, to come out and declare their position. Notice however, that he did not call out for those that were no longer loyal, rather, he asked those that "*claimed*" to still be loyal to go through the camp and identify those who are NO longer loyal, and to kill them whether they be family or friend. He did this for two main reasons.

First, because one cannot serve two masters and if the Levites claimed they were still loyal, they must prove it by forsaking their allegiance to any other masters.

Secondly, Moses was never in the camp when the uprising began for the golden calf to be built. Moses understood that some core people would have incited the uprising and others would have merely followed because they could not lead themselves. Asking the Levites to identify the real perpetrators was the appropriate way of identifying the core disloyal causers of the uprising.

This prevented him from blindly killing those who were mere followers as opposed to real instigators. This is a crucial lesson to learn as a business man or the leader of an organisation – that not everybody in the rioting crowd is guilty, some of them are simply following because they cannot lead themselves – they are corrupted but can still be used.

These challenges to loyalty will come, but remember that not everybody will be part of the group who incited the uprising and show of disloyalty. Secondly, be sure that you make a clear roll call to determine publicly who is still loyal to the cause or otherwise. This will give you a clear picture of what you are up against.

Finally, Moses ensures that their loyalty is rewarded. It is a principle. If disloyalty has a price, loyalty should too.

Otherwise, those who choose to remain loyal might think it unprofitable to have done so and this could increase the likelihood of them subsequently defecting to the disloyal camp.

Principle 19

BUILDING STRONG ORGANISATIONAL CULTURES

Genesis 11: 1 – 9

Now the whole earth had one language and one speech. 2 And it came to pass, as they journeyed from the east, that they found a plain in the land of Shinar, and they dwelt there. 3 Then they said to one another, "Come, let us make bricks and bake them thoroughly." They had brick for stone, and they had asphalt for mortar. 4 And they said, "Come, let us build ourselves a city, and a tower whose top is in the heavens; let us make a name for ourselves, lest we be scattered abroad over the face of the whole earth." 5 But the Lord came down to see the city and the tower which the sons of men had built. 6 And the Lord said, "Indeed the people are one and they all have one language, and this is what they begin to do; now nothing that they propose to do will be withheld from them. 7 Come, let Us go down and there confuse their language, that they may not understand one another's speech." 8 So the Lord scattered them abroad from there over the face of all the earth, and they ceased building the city. 9 Therefore its name is called Babel, because there the Lord confused the language of all the earth; and from there the Lord scattered them abroad over the face of all the earth.

Language is not a physical thing only, it is a unifying spirit. Language as it is used here, if applied appropriately, is what sets apart an organisation to become the best at whatever it does.

Whether in business or leading a family or ministry, it should be a top priority to ensure everyone in your organisation speaks the same language. The language being referred to here is not the literal language we communicate in, but what defines you as a people.

It is the unified language of dressing; of the one vision to which everyone must commit; of how we all treat customers and our fellow workers; and of how we relate to each other. It is also the language of what we all believe in or of how we see and perceive risk and how we ought to consistently deal with it. It is all about building a *"language of how WE do things as a people"*.

The real power of language is its ability to unite a people, mentally, physically, psychologically and spiritually. In fact, the Hebrew word for language is *"saphah" which* also means *"binding"*.

Take any language, for example, and notice that in order to speak it and be understood by those who speak it, you need to pronounce the words and apply the phonetics in a *"fixed and particular"* way. Individuals DO NOT suddenly determine what pronunciation or phonetics they personally wish to use. This is NOT Dogma, on the contrary, it is the way we do things as a peculiar set of people. The crucial need in having the same *organisational language* is reflected in three benefits that can accrue from this, namely:

1. Firstly, if the people of your organisation speak the same language it helps to achieve results faster and more consistently. This is because for a people who speak the same language, instructions are more quickly understood in the same way by everybody. Little or no time is spent interpreting or correcting the errors caused by misinterpretations. This makes leadership very effective.

2. Secondly, an organisation that speaks the same language ensures that it is easily identifiable to external people. If people external to the organisation such as a potential convert, a customer or a supplier identifies your organisation as one in which the same language is spoken, they are likely to feel much more comfortable doing business with you. This is because they know that, irrespective of

whom they talk to in the organisation, they will most likely receive the same results, suggesting a high consistency of language throughout the organisation.

3. Finally, for an organisation or a people that speak the same language, it is very easy to spot the imposters or frauds who do not fit in. For business people, organisational and political leaders who will be employing people to work for them, it is crucial first, that you define your own language, and then ensure that when you recruit, you do not do so only based on skills but also on whether or not the one being recruited has a closer disposition towards your language.

   For example, if you are in an industry where customer care is of exceptional relevance to your business success, then you ought to understand that potential recruits would have come from different backgrounds. Not all of them therefore will have a natural or teachable disposition towards customer care. The best you can do for yourself is to hire those who are more closely disposed to your core language of customer care.

   Likewise for a political leader, the ideals you stand for represent your language – those, therefore, that form the core of your team should be people who have a closer disposition to speaking the same language of ideals.

Principle 20

BUILDING A 360 DEGREE CORPORATE VISION

Genesis 13: 10 – 18

*[10] And Lot lifted his eyes and saw all the plain of Jordan, that
it was well watered everywhere (before the Lord destroyed
Sodom and Gomorrah) like the garden of the Lord, like
the land of Egypt as you go toward Zoar. [11] Then Lot chose
for himself all the plain of Jordan, and Lot journeyed east.
And they separated from each other. [12] Abram dwelt in the
land of Canaan, and Lot dwelt in the cities of the plain
and pitched his tent even as far as Sodom. [13] But the men
of Sodom were exceedingly wicked and sinful against the
Lord. [14] And the Lord said to Abram, after Lot had separated from him: "Lift your eyes now and look from the
place where you are—northward, southward, eastward,
and westward; [15] for all the land which you see I give to
you and your descendants forever. [16] And I will make your
descendants as the dust of the earth; so that if a man could
number the dust of the earth, then your descendants also
could be numbered. [17] Arise, walk in the land through its
length and its width, for I give it to you." [18] Then Abram*

moved his tent, and went and dwelt by the terebinth trees of Mamre, which are in Hebron, and built an altar there to the Lord.

Abram ended up possessing more lands than Lot even though they both took turns to stand in the same place and to choose what they wanted. This is a crucial lesson in catching a vision that every business person or leader needs to have if they wish to go far.

Everybody can have a vision but not everybody's business, family, organisational or ministerial vision will yield abundance in all spheres of life. So how do you look into the future and tap into yet unknown success?

Note this from the passage: both men looked in front of them; that is, they both stood on "*today*" and looked ahead of them into "*tomorrow*". The first principle of visioning is this – you cannot achieve what you have not seen. It is a spiritual and universal law. It will work for the sinner as well as the saved. What you see is what you get - nothing more, nothing less.

But here is the secret of why Abram became a greater possessor than Lot. Firstly, they both lifted their eyes, but note that "*Lot lifted his eyes*" whereas in Abram's case, God told him to "*lift and look*".

Lot looked up in his humanness and as such, could only

see in one direction. Even physically speaking, no one can possibly turn their eyes round enough to see everything before, beside and behind at the same time. But by involving God in Abram's case – (who sees all things and knows all things), Abram was able to tap into the seeing power of God and as a result, received an all-round view of what possibilities lay on every side for the taking.

In other words, as a visionary leader, you need to at all times have a three hundred and sixty degree awareness of the opportunities around your business, organisation or family – and you cannot do this by your strength – it takes the eye of God.

Until you see ALL the opportunities to choose from, you may end up like Lot who thought his opportunity looked like the Garden of Eden, but in fact it was not – it was the way to Sodom!

Also bear in mind, Lot had to leave before *God asked Abraham to look up and see.* If you will locate viable opportunities all around you and not just in front of you like, you need to separate yourself from any obstructive noise, choking competition or anything that is likely to cloud your judgement or vision. Lot is indeed everything that clouds the clarity of your vision. Therefore, it does not mean ignore it, but removing it completely out of your line of vision so you can see things more clearly and covering a wider scope.

Principle 21

CONVERTING ENQUIRERS INTO LOYAL FOLLOWERS

Genesis 41: 17 - 36

*17 Then Pharaoh said to Joseph: "Behold, in my dream I
stood on the bank of the river. 18 Suddenly seven cows came
up out of the river, fine looking and fat; and they fed in the
meadow. 19 Then behold, seven other cows came up after
them, poor and very ugly and gaunt, such ugliness as I have
never seen in all the land of Egypt. 20 And the gaunt and
ugly cows ate up the first seven, the fat cows. 21 When they
had eaten them up, no one would have known that they
had eaten them, for they were just as ugly as at the beginning. So I awoke. 22 Also I saw in my dream, and suddenly
seven heads came up on one stalk, full and good. 23 Then
behold seven heads, withered, thin, and blighted by the east
wind, sprang up after them. 24 And the thin heads devoured
the seven good heads. So I told this to the magicians, but
there was no one who could explain it to me." 25 Then Joseph
said to Pharaoh, "The dreams of Pharaoh are one; God
has shown Pharaoh what He is about to do: 26 The seven
good cows are seven years, and the seven good heads are*

*seven years; the dreams are one. [27] And the seven thin and
ugly cows which came up after them are seven years, and
the seven empty heads blighted by the east wind are seven
years of famine. [28] This is the thing which I have spoken to
Pharaoh. God has shown Pharaoh what He is about to do.
[29] Indeed seven years of great plenty will come throughout
all the land of Egypt; [30] but after them seven years of famine
will arise, and all the plenty will be forgotten in the land
of Egypt; and the famine will deplete the land. [31] So the
plenty will not be known in the land because of the famine
following, for it will be very severe. [32] And the dream was
repeated to Pharaoh twice because the thing is established
by God, and God will shortly bring it to pass. [33] "Now therefore, let Pharaoh select a discerning and wise man, and
set him over the land of Egypt. [34] Let Pharaoh do this, and
let him appoint officers over the land, to collect one-fifth
of the produce of the land of Egypt in the seven plentiful
years. [35] And let them gather all the food of those good years
that are coming, and store up grain under the authority of
Pharaoh, and let them keep food in the cities. [36] Then that
food shall be as a reserve for the land for the seven years of
famine which shall be in the land of Egypt, that the land
may not perish during the famine."*

The principle gleaned from this passage will help you consistently achieve two things. Firstly, it will help you sell yourself or anything else without necessarily marketing it. Secondly, it will help you, without fail, convert opportunities from possibility to reality; or if you are in the business of people, it will always convert potential customers or contacts into loyal followers.

Here is Joseph pulled from the dungeon to do only one thing – interpret Pharaoh's dream. But what does he do? He acknowledges first of all that he is not by himself, but has the backing of heaven – God. By that, he establishes the authority with which he achieves his excellent degree of efficiency. He makes Pharaoh understand from the start that though he may not wear a robe and a crown, yet his skills and abilities have the backing of God – a king higher than Pharaoh. By establishing this, Joseph settles it in Pharaoh's mind that he had a verifiable, authoritative and respected qualification to assure him *(Pharaoh)* that whatever he *(Joseph)* was about to say was nothing short of authentic.

Next, Joseph proceeds to interpret Pharaoh's dream; but he did not stop there – he follows with the third level: he also provides a fool-proof practical solution.

This three pronged approach is excellent for dealing with

every opportunity that presents itself first in the form of an enquiry *(be it a lost soul, a potential customer, investor, family, followers, employee, whatsoever).*

It allows you to first establish why you are best suited person to answer the enquiry; then you provide an answer to the enquiry; and finally, go a step beyond and provide a an additional, potentially needed (but not requested) information or solution that has a very high chance of benefiting the enquirer.

The first two steps allow you to gain the confidence of the inquirer and assure them that you are the best suited person for whatever information or resource they need and that you are able to provide it. The final stage shows that, apart delivering what was requested of you, you also have potentially more solutions beyond the current requirement.

A person may not become a loyal customer or follower immediately, but they will always remember that you were the source of solutions beyond what they requested, and so, in time, they will find their way back to you.

Principle 22

WHAT YOU SAY IS WHAT YOU GET...

Genesis 2: 19 – 20

[19] Out of the ground the Lord God formed every beast of the field and every bird of the air, and brought them to Adam to see what he would call them. And whatever Adam called each living creature, that was its name. [20] So Adam gave names to all cattle, to the birds of the air, and to every beast of the field. But for Adam there was not found a helper comparable to him.

Being a leader or the head of a business puts you in a unique position. Spiritually speaking, your voice becomes the voice of the organisation, home or any other unit you are leading.

It is a *"grace"* that automatically comes upon a Godly leader. By this unique grace, what you speak concerning your unit, organisation or company has the power to bring it good or bad fortune. In the text above *"beasts"* are usually symbolic of troubles, dangerous people, unhappy, evil circumstances, contentious issues etc. So too, the *"birds of the air"* are symbolic of good people and fortune; pleasant, successful, joyful circumstances; or generally events that come to lift you high.

Here is the interesting part – *"whatever Adam called each living creature, that was its name."* The original Hebrew text reads differently and much more correctly. This is what it says: *"whatever Adam declared it to be, that is what it became"*. The difference is enormous. It was not just a name Adam was giving them, he was declaring what their nature was to be from hence – it was certainly more than a name.

Adam was the head, grace was upon him and whatever he declared each animal to be, that *"became its nature"* under his leading. In other words, the lion may have originally come to him meek and timid, but by virtue of the declaration he made, it became the majestic king of the wild beasts.

Here is a fascinating example: the dog, as we all know it, was certainly a *beast of the field* – wild and dangerous. All of them. Adam named or declared it to be called *"Kelev"*. This is a Hebrew word that is made of two separate words *"Ke"* which means *"close to"* and *"Lev" which* means *"heart"*. Put them together and the word dog actually means *"close to man's heart."* Do you think it may be mere coincidence dogs, out of all the animals created, remains man's best friend?

The main point from this is that as a leader you will inevitably face challenging or joyful circumstances in the form of coming face to face with leadership *"beasts of the field"* or leadership *"birds of the air"*. However, what you call its name or declare it to be is what it will become from that point onwards. It is not really about the form in which it comes, but what you declare it to become after you have seen it.

Remember that *"life and death are in the power of the tongue"* – give life always and sustain life in your leadership and business by your declarations.

Principle 23

BRINGING OTHERS ALONG

Luke 14: 15 – 24

15 Now when one of those who sat at the table with Him
heard these things, he said to Him, "Blessed is he who shall
eat bread[a] in the kingdom of God!" 16 Then He said to
him, "A certain man gave a great supper and invited many,
17 and sent his servant at supper time to say to those who
were invited, 'Come, for all things are now ready.' 18 But they
all with one accord began to make excuses. The first said
to him, 'I have bought a piece of ground, and I must go
and see it. I ask you to have me excused.' 19 And another
said, 'I have bought five yoke of oxen, and I am going to test
them. I ask you to have me excused.' 20 Still another said, 'I
have married a wife, and therefore I cannot come.' 21 So that
servant came and reported these things to his master. Then
the master of the house, being angry, said to his servant,
'Go out quickly into the streets and lanes of the city, and
bring in here the poor and the maimed and the lame and
the blind.' 22 And the servant said, 'Master, it is done as you
commanded, and still there is room.' 23 Then the master said

to the servant, 'Go out into the highways and hedges, and compel them to come in, that my house may be filled. [24] *For I say to you that none of those men who were invited shall taste my supper.'"*

Have you ever heard the saying that *"every journey begins with one step"*? Maybe you may have also heard that *"the greatest failure of any man is the failure of not trying."*

The point being made is that the greatest time of any institution or business is its birth. If there is no birthing, then the issues of growth, success, fulfilment and greatness, among other things, do not even come into the picture.

Having established this premise, let me also say that if a man does not believe in your beginning enough to honour it, then he has no part in your latter glory.

Many get it wrong in believing that the point at which one begins to be recognized and garnished with all manner of medals for their various achievements, is really the pinnacle. On the contrary, your pinnacle is when you first recognised that you had it in you to start that business, lead that institution, climb the ladder of power or begin a family.

The beginning, which many consider the lowest point, is in fact the highest - that is the point at which you looked at the little seed in your hand and chose to see a big tree instead.

The people you give an opportunity to see and celebrate the seed in your hands who turned you down in the hope that, they will celebrate with you when the real "tree" grows into manifestation – they have no business standing under the tree with you when it eventually grows; because to them, that tree will always be nothing more than a seed which can either be fed to the birds or trampled under foot.

Principle 24

OPTIMISING THE USE OF ADVISORY SERVICES

Acts 3: 1 – 10

Now Peter and John went up together to the temple at the hour of prayer, the ninth hour. [2] And a certain man lame from his mother's womb was carried, whom they laid daily at the gate of the temple which is called Beautiful, to ask alms from those who entered the temple; [3] who, seeing Peter and John about to go into the temple, asked for alms. [4] And fixing his eyes on him, with John, Peter said, "Look at us." [5] So he gave them his attention, expecting to receive something from them. [6] Then Peter said, "Silver and gold I do not have, but what I do have I give you: In the name of Jesus Christ of Nazareth, rise up and walk." [7] And he took him by the right hand and lifted him up, and immediately his feet and ankle bones received strength. [8] So he, leaping up, stood and walked and entered the temple with them—walking, leaping, and praising God. [9] And all the people saw him walking and praising God. [10] Then they knew that it was he who sat begging alms at the Beautiful Gate of the temple; and they were filled with wonder and amazement at what had happened to him.

❧ ❧ ❧

A very fundamental leadership principle is that a man cannot give what he does not have. If understood in its entirety, this should help anyone optimize results from any activity or relationship and to properly manage their expectations.

John and Peter at this time had a consistent record of a healing ministry. They did not struggle to effect healing miracle by the power of God. It was a gift they knew they had. Everything else the beggar was asking for, they did not have. But because they understood this principle, they spoke to the beggar to get him to align his expectations with what they were capable of delivering to him.

In terms of maximising results, this principle should be a guide in determining who we go to for solutions. In other words, if you are looking to someone or an institution for a solution which they are incapable of providing, then you are not seeking to optimize their involvement with you.

Interestingly, although God makes different people available to us in our times of need, only a handful of these people will provide optimal solutions. To optimally manage these relationships therefore means recognizing how best each of these people fit into satisfying our needs.

The other thing the passage speaks about is specialisation

– what we are best at makes it easier to sustain our lead and superiority in that area. This is the reason why some businesses, after many years of dabbling in new and different things and being unprofitable, go back to the one thing they are good at and stick with it.

Combining these two insights, we can now properly gauge what to expect from people or identifying who is best placed to help our needs. This applies not only to people but also to systems, organisations and products. The bottom line is this – the person or system best placed to meet your need is

(i) one that exhibits the solution you are seeking for naturally or as a standard *(i.e. it must not be under any form of pressure, manipulation or by-action)*
(ii) the solution they are exhibiting *(which you are looking for)* should be one they do consistently.

This approach to determining who or what system you approach for solutions to your needs (in prayer of course) should be underlined by the fact that:

(i) you have clearly defined what your needs are
(ii) you have clearly define what constitutes a long-lasting solution to your needs

Remember, nobody or system can give to you what they do not have.

Principle 25

LEADERSHIP TALENT + DELEGATION = GROWTH

Acts 6: 1 – 7

Now in those days, when the number of the disciples was multiplying, there arose a complaint against the Hebrews by the Hellenists, because their widows were neglected in the daily distribution. [2] Then the twelve summoned the multitude of the disciples and said, "It is not desirable that we should leave the word of God and serve tables. [3] Therefore, brethren, seek out from among you seven men of good reputation, full of the Holy Spirit and wisdom, whom we may appoint over this business; [4] but we will give ourselves continually to prayer and to the ministry of the word." [5] And the saying pleased the whole multitude. And they chose Stephen, a man full of faith and the Holy Spirit, and Philip, Prochorus, Nicanor, Timon, Parmenas, and Nicolas, a proselyte from Antioch, [6] whom they set before the apostles; and when they had prayed, they laid hands on them. [7] Then the word of God spread, and the number of the disciples multiplied greatly in Jerusalem, and a great many of the priests were obedient to the faith.

No man was created an island. This verse teaches a valuable lesson about leadership, business and the exercise of power in the form of talent identification and delegation. It teaches that identifying talent combined with delegation can bring astonishing results. Interestingly, delegation of authority is one of the most difficult things to do.

Let us examine the passage above to see the three major expansions that were achieved as a result of delegation. They were:

(1) Then the word of God spread – growth of the vision
(2) The number of the disciples multiplied greatly –increased following
(3) A great many of the priests were obedient to the faith – internal alignment and loyalty.

One of the major challenges with delegation is how it is done. Before we delve into what the scripture teaches about the *"how"* of delegation, it is worth noting that to delegate does not mean the delegator is weak, inadequate or incapable. Rather, it means you have the ability to trust in the potential abilities of others, leading to them respecting you more for believing in them.

In truth, delegation is also the most subtle form of control in that it fosters allegiance. It is a non-verbal way of communicating to the other person that "*I am not delegating because I cannot do it, I'm delegating because I would like you to rise up and occupy where I currently am, because I am about to move up.*"

Now, let's look at the things to consider if you want to delegate in the most appropriate way:

(1) ***"It is not desirable that we should leave the word of God and serve tables"*** – you first need to recognize as a leader, what things you need to keep doing and what things you can delegate. Understand that not everything can be delegated. The simplest way to understand this is to ask yourself if an issue, activity or event will directly affect the achievement of the CORE objectives of the business or organisation, then it should not be delegated.

For example, in the biblical passage above, the core objective was winning souls through the preaching of the gospel and social care of new converts. Although serving tables was a complimentary welfare service to complete the entire service of winning souls to Christ, the former *(preaching the word)*, directly affects the primary objective of winning souls, whereas the latter *(serving new converts food)* would not. As such, preaching the gospel could not be delegated but serving at tables was.

(2) ***"Men of good reputation"*** – the person to whom the task is being delegated must have a good reputation. The big question is *"a reputation in what?"* You need to understand that whoever you are delegating to is more or less a representative of you, so you need to know what specific type of *"good reputation"* is needed for the kind of assignment you are about to delegate. For example, does it require charisma, a particular technical skill, diplomacy, patience, strategic foresight or certain organisational ability? And does the potential delegate have a consistent reputation in it?

(3) ***"Full of the Holy Spirit"*** – You will stand a better chance of success if you are able to delegate to someone who fears God and is filled with the Holy Spirit than someone who lacks both. If the delegate has relationship with the Holy Spirit, then your delegation is even doubly secure – because in your absence, the delegate can still receive spot on directions directly from the Holy Spirit who knows all things. The Holy Spirit can also supervise their operations and report back to you by revelation, what has been happening in your absence.

(4) ***"Full of wisdom":*** whoever you delegate to must at least know something about the task they are being called upon to perform. Do not be naïve and make the mistake of thinking they will grow into it. Teaching or training someone to

do something is totally different from delegating it to them and expecting the job still done to a standard close enough to what you would have delivered yourself.

(5) ***"Whom they set before the apostles; and when they had prayed, they laid hands on them"*** – delegation is not a thing to be taken lightly, whenever you delegate a responsibility, you need to also release the authority to go with it. This is symbolized by the apostles laying their hands on the chosen men – it symbolizes to all who were present, that the delegates were not only commissioned but have been given the full seal of apostles' authority, to act on the latter's behalf.

Principle 26

THE IMPORTANCE OF COMMUNICATION

1 Corinthians 2: 6 – 16

6 However, we speak wisdom among those who are mature, yet not the wisdom of this age, nor of the rulers of this age, who are coming to nothing. 7 But we speak the wisdom of God in a mystery, the hidden wisdom which God ordained before the ages for our glory, 8 which none of the rulers of this age knew; for had they known, they would not have crucified the Lord of glory. 9 But as it is written: "Eye has not seen, nor ear heard, nor have entered into the heart of man the things which God has prepared for those who love Him." 10 But God has revealed them to us through His Spirit. For the Spirit searches all things, yes, the deep things of God. 11 For what man knows the things of a man except the spirit of the man which is in him? Even so no one knows the things of God except the Spirit of God. 12 Now we have received, not the spirit of the world, but the Spirit who is from God, that we might know the things that have been freely given to us by God. 13 These things we also speak, not in words which man's wisdom teaches but which the Holy Spirit teaches, comparing spiritual things with spiritual. [14] But the natural man does not receive the things of the Spirit of God, for they are foolishness to him; nor can he know them, because they are spiritually discerned. [15] But he who is spiritual judges all things, yet he himself is rightly judged by no one. [16] For "who has known the mind of the Lord that he may instruct Him?" But we have the mind of Christ.

Events that have occurred over the many years show the knowledge of man is very limited. Consider basic things like our attempts to tell the weather accurately all the time – it doesn't always work according to our estimations.

Now consider then similar scenarios that play out in daily business and leadership; scenarios involving the coming together of very many complex human and non-human factors all at once and you will realise that we face an even more difficult task getting it right every time as leaders or generally in business.

For godly people doing business, leading or exercising power, it is a forgone conclusion that the daily knowledge you need to run your entity effectively is the knowledge and the wisdom of God. You need the Holy Spirit kind of knowledge that takes you into the future before you get there – this is not mere "forecasting" of future events – it is actual future events brought to your knowledge that shows you all the parameters to consider before you make decisions. This is a kind of supernatural intelligence that brings to your attention timely and relevant information in a form you will not usually find in the human realm.

The truth is the major difference between the success and failure of two similar businesses, leaders or power brokers is the comprehensiveness and accuracy of information each possesses. So I ask: what better source to procure the past, present and future knowledge than from God who created the past, present and future?

That having been said, I too am a Christian, yet I cannot discount the need for leaders and business people to learn the art of *"Critical Thinking."* It is this natural disposition to deep thinking *(which can be learnt)* combined with, combined with the supernatural *"insight and foresight"* of the Holy Spirit that makes us unstoppable. The truth sages alone have known for centuries is this – God, does not give wisdom and understanding to a man who has not endowed himself with knowledge.

Otherwise if the almighty God, through the Holy Spirit were to deliver a certain wisdom or insight about the future to a businessman or leader, HOW would he deploy it for an extended good except he has knowledge?

Principle 27

BALANCING POWER WITHIN AN ORGANIZATION

1 Corinthians 3: 5 – 15

*5 Who then is Paul, and who is Apollos, but ministers
through whom you believed, as the Lord gave to each one?
6 I planted, Apollos watered, but God gave the increase. 7 So
then neither he who plants is anything, nor he who waters,
but God who gives the increase. 8 Now he who plants and
he who waters are one, and each one will receive his own
reward according to his own labour. 9 For we are God's
fellow workers; you are God's field, you are God's building.
10 According to the grace of God which was given to me, as a
wise master builder I have laid the foundation, and another
builds on it. But let each one take heed how he builds on it.
11 For no other foundation can anyone lay than that which
is laid, which is Jesus Christ. 12 Now if anyone builds on this
foundation with gold, silver, precious stones, wood, hay,
straw, 13 each one's work will become clear; for the Day will
declare it, because it will be revealed by fire; and the fire will
test each one's work, of what sort it is. 14 If anyone's work
which he has built on it endures, he will receive a reward.*

[15] *If anyone's work is burned, he will suffer loss; but he himself will be saved, yet so as through fire.*

A fundamental rule for maintaining power or maintaining the concentration of institutional authority, is to consciously ensure that no one person or department within the organisation becomes overly indispensable – no one unit should become the pivot on which the entire organisation tilts.

If this happens, the organisation is likely to be held hostage by such a department or person. There are several ways one can orchestrate the re-alignment of power and regain control, if it is already a problem:

(i) One practical way to achieve this is to dilute the current central power or authority in the person or unit by adding other persons or units to assist in carrying out their tasks. This way, the decision to hold the entity to ransom, whether consciously or otherwise no more rests in one or a few hands. Keep the task the same, dilute the number of persons or units with responsibility for those tasks,

(ii) Another method is the direct opposite of the above – maintain the number of persons or units with responsibility for sensitive tasks of the entity, but dilute their immediate power or authority by splitting or reducing the tasks they are responsible for. The aim is the same – dilution.

From the scripture, you will find two fundamental ways of assessing whether too much power or authority is being concentrated in one person or department.

First - when a person or a unit refuses or finds it hard to build on someone else's foundation. Alternatively, they may build the foundation but not want anyone else to build on it. In other words, they get accustomed to focusing more on their individual selves or units at the expense of the entire team or organisation. This is a sign that they feel indispensable to the organisation.

Another indication a unit or person within an organisation is beginning to feel indispensable is when they indiscriminately start wanting to re-do the tasks or requesting for a mark-down of the input of other people or units, because they feel it does not meet their standards. In short, they are trying to set their standards above and beside organisational standards that may already exist.

Even as the scripture says *"the fire shall test each man's work"* – if any team or person within a business or organisation does not want its activities or work to be reviewed or questioned in anyway, it is certainly growing bigger than the business or organisation itself and this is another clear sign that they consider themselves to be indispensable.

Principle 28

REPUTATIONAL RISK MANAGEMENT

1 Corinthians 6: 12 – 20

[12] All things are lawful for me, but all things are not helpful. All things are lawful for me, but I will not be brought under the power of any. [13] Foods for the stomach and the stomach for foods, but God will destroy both it and them. Now the body is not for sexual immorality but for the Lord, and the Lord for the body. [14] And God both raised up the Lord and will also raise us up by His power. [15] Do you not know that your bodies are members of Christ? Shall I then take the members of Christ and make them members of a harlot? Certainly not! [16] Or do you not know that he who is joined to a harlot is one body with her? For "the two," He says, "shall become one flesh." [17] But he who is joined to the Lord is one spirit with Him. [18] Flee sexual immorality. Every sin that a man does is outside the body, but he who commits sexual immorality sins against his own body. [19] Or do you not know that your body is the temple of the Holy Spirit who is in you, whom you have from God, and you are not your own? [20] For you were bought at a

price; therefore glorify God in your body and in your spirit, which are God's.

The world is not an isolated iceberg; neither does one's ability to do business directly with God exclude him/her from the need to collaborate with other businesses, leaders or power brokers.

Unfortunately, such necessary dependence means that your business, your leadership and your power is daily being exposed to the reputational risks of others.

A reputational risk means possibility of your reputation (i.e. good name, respected brand, enviable track record etc.) or that of your organisation being damaged, not by a deliberate act on your part, but by virtue of your necessary association with some other person or organisation whose image has been recklessly tarnished – i.e. simply by virtue of association.

It is like being branded a thief because of your association with people who happen to steal. Unfortunately, the attack on your reputation most likely won't be based on an objective inquiry into whether or not your involvement was deliberate or accidental, or whether your association was with genuine or criminal intent.

The situation can be likened to a man of good reputation who has a relationship with a harlot – a sexually immoral woman. Having a relationship with such a woman, without genuinely knowing she is a harlot, unfortunately does not prevent the good man's reputation from being tarnished by ignorant association.

The lesson – it is therefore essential that before you enter into any medium to long-term involvement with other persons or businesses, you make a conscious effort to seek God, and do some research so you will know to a reasonable degree of certainty the reputational risk to which you are likely to be exposing yourself.

Certainly, in my experience, the cost and time involved in seeking Godly counsel and checking the background facts leading to a potential relationship are far less than the damage that could occur if any reputational risk emerges.

It is worth understanding that re- building a tarnished reputation is certainly harder than trying to build one from scratch – sadly, once tarnished, one also loses the option to build from scratch.

Principle 29

A LESSON IN LONG-TERM HR MANAGEMENT

1 Corinthians 7: 17 – 24

[17] But as God has distributed to each one, as the Lord has called each one, so let him walk. And so I ordain in all the churches. [18] Was anyone called while circumcised? Let him not become uncircumcised. Was anyone called while uncircumcised? Let him not be circumcised. [19] Circumcision is nothing and uncircumcision is nothing, but keeping the commandments of God is what matters. [20] Let each one remain in the same calling in which he was called. [21] Were you called while a slave? Do not be concerned about it; but if you can be made free, rather use it. [22] For he who is called in the Lord while a slave is the Lord's freedman. Likewise he who is called while free is Christ's slave. [23] You were bought at a price; do not become slaves of men. [24] Brethren, let each one remain with God in that state in which he was called.

A very important philosophy in building a successful business, leadership or system of power is not to employ people and try to change them, but rather hire them as they are and with what they possess. In this way, you are taking note of what their overall qualifications and disposition can add to your organisation or self.

Individuals function better in their uniqueness – what has defined them up to the point you met them. Therefore, your prerogative when recruiting is to answer these crucial questions:

1. Would my business, my leadership and my power structure benefit by employing this person(s) in their current state of disposition?
2. If they never changed in the next couple of years, would they still be useful to the future direction of the business?

If you begin to think this way, you will make much more successful recruitments because, you would not be engaging in the conflicts associated with bringing in round pegs and attempting to shape them to fit your square holes.

Your leadership and organisation will be spared the frustration of having persons who are not changing to meet your evolving needs. Indeed, it is you who need to change your understanding of the recruitment process and who you should be employing.

From the passage above, it is God who has distributed talents and abilities to all men, so realistically, what each person has is simply a reflection of what has been distributed to them.

You will be trying to play God by employing someone who God has not given what it takes to satisfy YOUR needs, and then trying to change them forcefully to suit your demands.

What God did not distribute to them willingly, do not force them to reflect - you are NOT God and this is certainly not the best way to recruit staff.

Principle 30

ORGANIZATIONAL CHARITY

2 Corinthians 9: 6 – 12

6 But this I say: He who sows sparingly will also reap spar-
ingly, and he who sows bountifully will also reap bounti-
fully. 7 So let each one give as he purposes in his heart, not
grudgingly or of necessity; for God loves a cheerful giver.
8 And God is able to make all grace abound toward you,
that you, always having all sufficiency in all things, may
have abundance for every good work. 9 As it is written:
"He has dispersed abroad, He has given to the poor; His
righteousness endures forever." 10 Now may He who supplies
seed to the sower, and bread for food, supply and multi-
ply the seed you have sown and increase the fruits of your
righteousness, 11 while you are enriched in everything for
all liberality, which causes thanksgiving through us to God.
12 For the administration of this service not only supplies
the needs of the saints, but also is abounding through many
thanksgivings to God,

Giving to God and His work is not just something for individual Christians. It is one of those things for which it is easier to see the advantage as an individual but fail to see that it can work equal well for your business, organisation or whatever system of political power you are involved in.

There are generally three different levels of giving you should consider engaging in as a leader of your business or organisation in order to experience stability and growth.

Firstly, giving to the poor in your immediate community – what is now considered in the secular world as social responsibility is actually a form of giving instructed by scriptures. It is a Godly responsibility and not something that an organisation should do out of forced obligation – that is selfishness.

Secondly, giving to make impact abroad – Let your giving transcend beyond the shores of the country where you operate. I can understand that many leaders and businesses may not see a Christian basis for this, but there is one – i.e. sowing and reaping never ceases.

If you do not engage in this, it means you cannot expect to reap fruits from the lands into which your seed has not been sown. For example, if you have a business based in Africa and you are expecting business to flow to you from other countries globally, you need to be asking yourself, *"is my seed being sown in any of these lands?"* Perhaps, this may not be a realistic consideration on a country by country basis, but at least looking at this from a continental level would be reasonable, in my view – we simply cannot reap where we haven't sown.

I am not disputing that you may still get business from say America without sowing a seed in it, but the question is <u>whether</u> the benefits you gain from these lands are sustained and protected from misfortunes.

I would also personally recommend giving to charities that benefit the Jewish people directly, in order to take advantage of the Abrahamic blessing - *"I'll bless those who bless you."*

Many people make the mistake of saying, because Christians by faith are of the seed of Abraham, there really is not any distinction between the Christians and Jews anymore.

This is a very dangerous assumption to live by because the truth is, even though we are grafted in as sons of Abraham, the Jews, by blood and covenant right, are still the first line partakers of Abraham's prophetic blessings.

This is not the place for this kind of discussion, but I assure you giving to the Jews is something that works every time, without fail.

One of the secrets the very wealthy do not teach in their numerous books is that they disperse their seed abroad and the fruits abroad come to back them. If you doubt me, ask Slim Helu, Bill Gates or Richard Branson when you next see one of them.

Finally, your third level of giving should be one that connects you to righteousness – The church of Christ is the seat of righteousness in the earth and in order for your business or organisation to be continually engaged with the righteousness of God, it needs to give to the body of Christ or the church.

Here is something to keep in mind. God is business-minded and so He will not allow an organisation or business that regularly sustains His righteousness on earth to be destroyed or harmed, without cause by unrighteousness.

In effect, applying all these three levels of corporate giving allows your business and organisation to tap into local and international blessings in the physical as well as spiritual blessings all around – the Spirit of God has no boundaries.

Principle 31

FORMING STRATEGIC ALLIANCES

Joshua 2: 1 – 14

Now Joshua the son of Nun sent out two men from Acacia Grove to spy secretly, saying, "Go, view the land, especially Jericho." So they went, and came to the house of a harlot named Rahab, and lodged there. [2] And it was told the king of Jericho, saying, "Behold, men have come here tonight from the children of Israel to search out the country."[3] So the king of Jericho sent to Rahab, saying, "Bring out the men who have come to you, who have entered your house, for they have come to search out all the country."[4] Then the woman took the two men and hid them. So she said, "Yes, the men came to me, but I did not know where they were from. [5] And it happened as the gate was being shut, when it was dark, that the men went out. Where the men went I do not know; pursue them quickly, for you may overtake them." [6] (But she had brought them up to the roof and hidden them with the stalks of flax, which she had laid in order on the roof.) [7] Then the men pursued them by the road to the Jordan, to the fords. And as soon as those who pursued them had gone out, they shut the gate. [8] Now before they lay down, she came up to them on the roof, [9] and said to the men: "I know that the Lord has given you the land, that the terror of you has fallen on us, and that all the inhabitants of the land are fainthearted because of you. [10] For we have heard how the Lord dried up the water of the Red Sea for you when you came out of Egypt, and what you did to the two kings of the Amorites who were on the other side of the Jordan, Sihon and Og, whom you utterly destroyed. [11] And as soon as we heard these things, our hearts melted; neither did there remain any more courage in anyone because of you, for the Lord your God, He is God in heaven above and on earth beneath. [12] Now therefore, I beg you, swear to me by the Lord, since I have shown you kindness, that you also will show kindness to my father's house, and give me a true token, [13] and spare my father, my mother, my brothers, my sisters, and all that they have, and deliver our lives from death." [14] So the men answered her, "Our lives for yours, if none of you tell this business of ours. And it shall be, when the Lord has given us the land, that we will deal kindly and truly with you."

I may have talked about strategic alliances at some point in this book. Now, this passage emphasizes an important aspect of that – how to locate good allies in business or within organisations. Reading the Bible text, you realize that the spies sent to Jericho by Joshua did not just end up in Rahab's home by chance - "they came to her."

A lesson to learn from the entire passage is that one of the easiest ways to rout a competitor is to find ways of creating or finding some form of alliance with someone from inside that same organisation. It was a strategy used effectively by the intelligence services of several countries during the well-known cold war era.

If there is anything leaders and other power brokers ought to learn from government agencies it is this – the most powerful countries are those with the most dedicated and effective information gathering systems. Information is the key that gives you a distinct advantage when dealing with almost anyone, especially if you have more information about them than they assume you have. It is one of the most powerful weapons you can use for weakening a person or entity; again, especially if it is information they deem to be secret. Having said this, there are a few things you need to look out for in order to determine who the right person to seek as an ally is.

1. ***Rahab was a harlot*** – it has to be someone with no fixed allegiances to any one party. This is an essential quality in two ways. First, it should be clear to you from the start that when it comes to matters of loyalty and trust, this person has none. Secondly, they do not seem to pose a threat to your competitor. Generally speaking, the higher the degree of loyalty, the higher the risk of damage associated with defection and, hence, the higher the level of suspicion that will be applied to your target ally.

2. ***Rahab hid the spies*** – It must be someone willing to protect your identity, at least to the extent that the person also benefits from it.

3. ***Rahab told the soldiers to pursue and they did*** – it must be somebody your competitor listens to or who has some acceptable degree of influence. It does not have to be somebody with a very high level of authority, but somebody that the competitor finds believable. The reason why this is such a crucial characteristic is because it is one of the easiest methods by which you can sow diversions and create mis-directions in your competitor's organisation, just like how Rahab hid the spies and sent the soldiers on a wild goose chase.

4. ***Rahab "knew" Jericho was in the hands of Israel*** – your ally has got to be one who, to an extent, believes in your purpose and your ability to achieve success. But most crucially, if your ally does not believe that your success will also be benefit them, then they will not be willing to join your cause.

5. ***Rahab tells how fainthearted Jericho was*** – and this, I would say is one of the two most crucial pieces of information needed for Israel to succeed. Providing this necessary information about Jericho qualifies Rahab as a true ally.

   In truth, this is the core factor in any person qualifying for consideration as an ally – the ability to provide this kind of core information. Firstly, she discloses the emotional state of the men of Jericho, something that the spies never knew before. She tells them how terror has come upon them until they are fainthearted and their courage has left them. Any knowledge of the emotional state of your competition gives you an advantage in knowing whether they will be approaching the battle lines already defeated by or otherwise and how best to increase that psychological defeat (or mental pressure).

   This type of knowledge helps you to determine what resources you should commit to the process. By virtue of her strategic location on the high end of the walls of Jericho, she was able to provide a vantage point from which the spies could view Jericho and to assess the structural systems in place within Jericho, including the formations and orderliness of the soldiers as they ran out through the gates in empty pursuit. Seeing this from a business perspective, you are able to evaluate your competitor's technical infrastructure and manpower capabilities. These two factors demonstrate the importance of information and the type of ally you will need.

6. ***Rahab negotiated for the safety of her family*** – you MUST offer some form of incentive to motivate your ally to cooperate, but it should be one that satisfies you, otherwise it will not serve your purpose. Both of you want something, but the trade-off needs to be well balanced. Since the ally holds the key to vital information or strategic know-how you need, you should also have something of importance to offer that your ally wants so much that they are willing to make the exchange.

   What you are offering needs to be the kind of reward that you are certain the competitor cannot give. This becomes your leverage.

Principle 32

THE POWER OF OPERATIONAL MILESTONES

Joshua 4: 1 – 8

And it came to pass, when all the people had completely crossed over the Jordan, that the Lord spoke to Joshua, saying: [2] "Take for yourselves twelve men from the people, one man from every tribe, [3] and command them, saying, 'Take for yourselves twelve stones from here, out of the midst of the Jordan, from the place where the priests' feet stood firm. You shall carry them over with you and leave them in the lodging place where you lodge tonight.'" [4] Then Joshua called the twelve men whom he had appointed from the children of Israel, one man from every tribe; [5] and Joshua said to them: "Cross over before the ark of the Lord your God into the midst of the Jordan, and each one of you take up a stone on his shoulder, according to the number of the tribes of the children of Israel, [6] that this may be a sign among you when your children ask in time to come, saying, 'What do these stones mean to you?' [7] Then you shall answer them that the waters of the Jordan were cut off before the ark of the covenant of the Lord; when it crossed over the Jordan, the waters of the Jordan were cut off. And these stones shall be for a memorial to the children of Israel forever." [8] *And the children of Israel did so, just as Joshua commanded, and took up twelve stones from the midst of the Jordan, as the Lord had spoken to Joshua, according to the number of the tribes of the children of Israel, and carried them over with them to the place where they lodged, and laid them down there.*

Leaders should always bear in mind the need to establish memorials because they help to move everybody forward.

Imagine you were counting from one to a million and while doing this you were interrupted and so became distracted. The chances are that if you went back to counting, you may have forgotten where you had stopped. On the surface, it may appear as though it never really mattered as long as you continued counting, but the truth is if you are doing an important thing such as running a business, you will need to remember exactly where you last stopped in order to continue from there. If you re-started counting from lower point than where you actually stopped, you would not only lose valuable time, but you would have lost money too.

Conversely, if you re-started further ahead where you

actually stopped counting, you would not only have factored in a "double count" in the process, you are likely to get to the end of the count and realise you have to return to the spot of error to make corrections – and that makes it twice the journey.

For a lot of different reasons, it is essential in your leadership role, whether business or political, that you learn to celebrate the stages of your achievements. It will boost corporate morale more than any motivational speech can. Some people take the view you should wait until you get to the end of the journey to do this, but when the end is very far away, you need to consider ways to sustain the corporate motivation until the end is achieved. This will not happen by continually cracking your whip.

What a memorial also does is to give the employees a sense of intrinsic motivation. It also serves as a constant reminder that if they have made it this far, then they can make it to the end. Although the goal is far away and difficult to achieve, setting up memorials along the way to celebrate small successes: (i) renews lost motivation (ii) re-energizes workers to keep pushing forward (iii) it takes the eyes of your employees or followers off the distance yet to be covered and (iv) gives them some assurance that that some distance has been covered already and so the final destination can be reached too.

As to how or by what means you establish your memorial I leave to your creative imagination. In the case of the Israelites, they took stones from the middle of the Jordan they had just crossed – a reference to remind them of exactly what point in the middle of the Jordan they had once been.

I do not know what will work for you as different leaders and business owners, but if there are any rules of the thumbs, I would suggest you factor in the following into your adopted approach:

(i) First, ensure that everybody on the team is acknowledged and no one is considered as being better than another when celebration is going on – just as every tribe in Israel was asked to take a stone each to contribute to the building of the memorial..

(ii) Secondly, and by no means the least, the point of reference with respect to the achievements to date must be the same for all involved. Nothing should be done to make any team or persons in the corporation feel that even though they were part of the memorial, their contribution was less than others.

This can be deduced from the passage all the stones were picked the same place – at the feet of the Levite priests. One single point of reference.

Principle 33

USING HEAVEN'S SUPPORT SERVICES

Judges 6: 1 – 10

Then the children of Israel did evil in the sight of the Lord. So
the Lord delivered them into the hand of Midian for seven
years, [2] and the hand of Midian prevailed against Israel.
Because of the Midianites, the children of Israel made for
themselves the dens, the caves, and the strongholds which
are in the mountains. [3] So it was, whenever Israel had sown,
Midianites would come up; also Amalekites and the people
of the East would come up against them. [4] Then they would
encamp against them and destroy the produce of the earth
as far as Gaza, and leave no sustenance for Israel, neither
sheep nor ox nor donkey. [5] For they would come up with
their livestock and their tents, coming in as numerous as
locusts; both they and their camels were without number;
and they would enter the land to destroy it. [6] So Israel
was greatly impoverished because of the Midianites, and
the children of Israel cried out to the Lord. [7] And it came
to pass, when the children of Israel cried out to the Lord
because of the Midianites, [8] that the Lord sent a prophet to

the children of Israel, who said to them, "Thus says the Lord God of Israel: 'I brought you up from Egypt and brought you out of the house of bondage; [9] *and I delivered you out of the hand of the Egyptians and out of the hand of all who oppressed you, and drove them out before you and gave you their land.* [10] *Also I said to you, "I am the Lord your God; do not fear the gods of the Amorites, in whose land you dwell." But you have not obeyed My voice.'"*

It is worth understanding the seriousness of this passage. Let's note carefully that Israel was not lazy – they were always tilling, irrigating and watching over the farming grounds until harvest time. The only real problem was that their enemies were the ones doing the actual harvesting.

Let's bear in mind that Israel's enemies; the Midianites and Amalekites, had heard about Israel and what God had done for them in the past – sufficient to put enough fear into them and hence their defeat by Israel. But this was not the case this time.

There is a very fundamental lesson to learn here. There will be times when your personal hard work and input, mentally and physically, can neither yield nor preserve the expected fruits or the results of your labour. When such a situation arises, neither your past experiences nor laurels will suffice and you need to do what Israel did – cry out to the Lord and seek to hear from Him through the voice of a prophet.

Someone is likely to ask why not hear from God directly. Well, when you are frustrated by putting in your all and reaping nothing, you are likely to have difficulty hearing clearly from God. Therefore, it is plain wisdom that under such circumstances, you seek a true vessel of God who can both be spiritual enough to hear the voice of God, and human enough to communicate that voice to you in such a language and tone that reaches you clearly.

Principle 34

RAISING LEADERS OR DIGGING THEM OUT

Judges 6: 11-13, 15, 17, 36-40

[11] Now the Angel of the Lord came and sat under the terebinth tree which was in Ophrah, which belonged to Joash the Abiezrite, while his son Gideon threshed wheat in the winepress, in order to hide it from the Midianites. [12] And the Angel of the Lord appeared to him, and said to him, "The Lord is with you, you mighty man of valour!" [13] Gideon said to Him, "O my lord,[a] if the Lord is with us, why then has all this happened to us? And where are all His miracles which our fathers told us about, saying, 'Did not the Lord bring us up from Egypt?' But now the Lord has forsaken us and delivered us into the hands of the Midianites."

[15] So he said to Him, "O my Lord, how can I save Israel? Indeed my clan is the weakest in Manasseh, and I am the least in my father's house."

[17] Then he said to Him, "If now I have found favour in Your sight, then show me a sign that it is You who talk with me.

36 So Gideon said to God, "If You will save Israel by my hand
as You have said— 37 look, I shall put a fleece of wool on
the threshing floor; if there is dew on the fleece only, and
it is dry on all the ground, then I shall know that You will
save Israel by my hand, as You have said." 38 And it was
so. When he rose early the next morning and squeezed the
fleece together, he wrung the dew out of the fleece, a bowlful
of water. 39 Then Gideon said to God, "Do not be angry with
me, but let me speak just once more: Let me test, I pray,
just once more with the fleece; let it now be dry only on the
fleece, but on all the ground let there be dew." 40 And God
did so that night. It was dry on the fleece only, but there was
dew on all the ground.

Here in this passage God delivers to us one of the most comprehensive mechanisms for locating people with potential leadership abilities – unless, of course, you have no intention of strengthening your superiority. If you have any such intention however, you will most certainly come to the crossroads of needing to find people with leadership qualities.

Contrary to the different schools of thought, God shows us here that some of the qualities that make a person an excellent leader can be learned while others are inherent. I have often been asked the question if all the qualities of a leader can be found in any one person. More often than not I usually respond philosophically by saying that they were found in Gideon, a man of like passions like us.

But it really is a matter of choice whether you are willing to put in some work to find a "leader" or "just a worker." With Gideon, we note the following:

1. ***Gideon threshing wheat*** – he was not a lazy person. He needed to feed his father and the rest of his family so he was out threshing wheat in spite of the threat posed by the presence of the Midianites and Amalekites. He is not the kind of person who finds a reason not to employ his abilities – no excuses. In practical business or leadership, such a person does not give excuses for failures neither does he believe in chances or luck but rather in taking responsibility for both failures and successes.

2. ***"The angel told him "The Lord is with you"*** – the "you" is in the singular but Gideon's question is in the plural "......*if the lord is with US....*" indicating his team spirit. This is the kind of man who hardly leaves anyone behind. It is not difficult when talking to people to sense their oneness with everybody or their selfishness spirit that keeps them aloof from others. A person with a good team spirit always ensures that people working with him

and for him are always adding value to themselves because when he goes up, he wants everybody else to do so along with him.

3. ***He was called a mighty man of valour*** – the qualities here represent strength and courage – the very qualities God and Moses required from Joshua in order for him to be successful. Possession of these traits means you have the ability not to waiver to the left or to the right in the midst of strong winds, but to proceed with a single focus toward a set goal until success is achieved. Being strong and courageous is not the same as being fool-hardy and stubborn. Instead, it is about identifying a destination and committing to journey there with the clear understanding that there will be obstacles of various kinds along the way, but you will not be deterred until success is achieved. For a leader, every decision made should have the final goal in mind and NOT based on the temporary occurrences on the journey.

4. ***"Why then has all this happened to us?"*** Gideon asks questions. To be very clear about what he was being called to do, he asked at least four questions. It is often true that those who ask questions are those who find answers – and leadership is all about asking the right questions in order

to have the right answers. From a spiritual perspective, it is also worth noting that God is in the business of giving answers because we as humans ought to be in the business of asking questions. Every great accomplishment in the world has resulted from someone providing a solution to the needs of mankind. Those who provide such solutions are, without doubt, people who have ask questions.

5. ***"My clan is the weakest in Manasseh**, and I am the least in my father's house"* – he had a realistic view of his true condition. Most people misinterpret faith to mean being blinded to reality. Here, Gideon is not self-deceived about his ranking and abilities.

He first assesses his current position. What he was really doing was asking God how to move from his current impoverished state to accomplish what God was asking of him. And God, who understood his question, answers him by saying *"it will happen by ME going with you"*.

A potential leader needs the ability to assess current conditions BUT not dwell on them. He does not let the current conditions hinder him, but rather help him measure the distance he has to travel and the best mode of moving from one point to the other. In short, he is a planner.

It is sad that many Christian leaders, in the name of "faith", venture unsuccessfully into business and leadership positions by blindly believing that God will catch them midway if they simply throw themselves in. They seem to forget that God is NOT a magician either.

6. ***"Then he said to Him, "If now I have found favour** in Your sight, then show me a sign". Here* Gideon is seeking to seal a deal with God. He does not want to proceed any further until a firm agreement is negotiated and reached. So many times leaders undertake a task, assuming that an understanding has been arrived at and never seeking formal proof of this until they come to the end and realize that things were not what they believed. – A good leader never takes anything for granted and, even when dealing with God, Gideon takes nothing for granted. The deal has to be sealed to make sure that the results are guaranteed. If God had failed (which won't happen) – Joshua would have referred Him to the "sign".

7. ***Next, this is what Gideon does** – "So Gideon went in and prepared a young goat and unleavened bread from an ephah of flour".* Two things he exemplifies here that should be present in every leadership candidate. Firstly, he had a heart of gratitude. Any leader who has no heart of gratitude can never recognize growth or accomplishment in anyone but himself. By offering a gift to the angel,

Gideon demonstrates that he understands that everything comes at a price, one way or the other. Truth is, if you cannot recognize the value of something, you cannot pay the right price for it, and if you cannot exercise the right price, you cannot own it. Persons with this quality not only get the job done, they ensure that the results are lasting by paying the full price.

8. ***Finally, in verses 36-40 of the*** text, we see Gideon exhibiting a very outstanding quality – the ability to consider issues from a holistic or 360 degree perspective. He does not only request for the fleece to be wet (the sign), but also being dry. A leadership candidate with this type of quality provides assurance that he is not short-sighted when it comes to deciding between options, and that he is sure to review each of his options back and forth and consider all angles of a decision to be made.

Principle 35

RISK MANAGEMENT ISSUES

Judges 11: 34 – 40

34 When Jephthah came to his house at Mizpah, there was his daughter, coming out to meet him with timbrels and dancing; and she was his only child. Besides her he had neither son nor daughter. 35 And it came to pass, when he saw her, that he tore his clothes, and said, "Alas, my daughter! You have brought me very low! You are among those who trouble me! For I have given my word to the Lord, and I cannot go back on it." 36 So she said to him, "My father, if you have given your word to the Lord, do to me according to what has gone out of your mouth, because the Lord has avenged you of your enemies, the people of Ammon." 37 Then she said to her father, "Let this thing be done for me: let me alone for two months, that I may go and wander on the mountains and bewail my virginity, my friends and I." 38 So he said, "Go." And he sent her away for two months; and she went with her friends, and bewailed her virginity on the mountains. 39 And it was so at the end of two months that she returned to her father, and he carried out his vow with her which he had vowed. She knew no man. And it became a custom in Israel [40] *that the daughters of Israel went four days each year to lament the daughter of Jephthah the Gileadite.*

A very straightforward lesson to learn from this passage is that you should only commit to actions whose outcomes you have some certainty about.

It is OK to take risks – but there are two main types of risk: there is one that you don't know anything whatsoever about the possible outcomes and there's another that you don't know all you should know about the possible outcomes. The latter, we can say, still has some degree of certainty about it. Let's consider a few rules of the thumb in dealing with risk:

1. Don't ever assume that numbers or volumes will always guarantee a specific expected outcome;
2. An action is already disastrous if you have reasonable uncertainties about both the inputs and the outcomes;
3. If you envisage the combination of an uncertain input with a possibly certain outcome or vice versa, the result is either a neutral, certain or an uncertain occurrence.

Jephthah possessed a large number of animals and servants (volumes and numbers) and so, by his human assessment, the chances of his daughter coming out first to meet him were extremely slim. What he failed to realise was that while he had control over what he could do with his servants and animals, he had no control over their free-will and that of his daughter. From this we learn that in order to manage risks – you must know the exact scope of your control.

From passage, we also learn that *you cannot commit what you do not control fully* because it will become an uncertainty in your decision making.

Principle 36

FINDING FAVOUR & LOCATING OPPORTUNITIES

Ruth 2: 1-8, 3:10-11

There was a relative of Naomi's husband, a man of great wealth, of the family of Elimelech. His name was Boaz. [2] So Ruth the Moabitess said to Naomi, "Please let me go to the field, and glean heads of grain after him in whose sight I may find favour." And she said to her, "Go, my daughter." [3] Then she left, and went and gleaned in the field after the reapers. And she happened to come to the part of the field belonging to Boaz, who was of the family of Elimelech. [4] Now behold, Boaz came from Bethlehem, and said to the reapers, "The Lord be with you!" And they answered him, "The Lord bless you!" [5] Then Boaz said to his servant who was in charge of the reapers, "Whose young woman is this?" [6] So the servant who was in charge of the reapers answered and said, "It is the young Moabite woman who came back with Naomi from the country of Moab. [7] And she said, 'Please let me glean and gather after the reapers among the sheaves.' So she came and has continued from morning until now, though she rested a little in the house." [8] Then Boaz said to

Ruth, "You will listen, my daughter, will you not? Do not go to glean in another field, nor go from here, but stay close by my young women.

[10] Then he said, "Blessed are you of the Lord, my daughter! For you have shown more kindness at the end than at the beginning, in that you did not go after young men, whether poor or rich. [11] And now, my daughter, do not fear. I will do for you all that you request, for all the people of my town know that you are a virtuous woman.

Many read the story of Ruth, the Moabite, and unanimously arrive at the conclusion that the story portrays valuable lessons about loyalty. I believe this – but it also teaches another important lesson about creating and seizing opportunities when they arise.

Verse two of the second chapter of Ruth says:

"Please let me go to the field, and glean heads of grain after him in whose sight I may find favour." Favour is one of the most effective means of moving from a position of disadvantage to an advantageous one without incurring the "*USUAL COST*". I often say to people in leadership that being in a certain "high position" is no guarantee that you can succeed in your endeavours all alone – everybody needs somebody; some more than others.

Sometimes we need to work with and through people to get from one point to the next. This could entail hard work over long periods. At other times, you can work with one or a smaller number of persons who move you very quickly in leaps from the beginning to the end in a shorter than usual time. This, I see as favour.

In the above passage, Ruth shows how this kind of favour actually works, and in so doing, shatters the contrary thinking of many, who believe that favour comes by waiting passively, rather than by engaging yourself in its pursuit.

"There was a relative of Naomi's husband, a man of great wealth, of the family of Elimelech. His name was Boaz". Firstly, Naomi accurately identifies who had the favour she needed change she and her daughter-in-law's life. In order to do this she had to assess her own needs before correctly determining who, out of her many relatives had the means to move her from her current impoverished status to a state of plenty. The qualities of Boaz are clearly stated by the scriptures:

(i) ***Firstly,*** ***he is a relative -*** so Boaz would have a better understanding of the family she found herself in and would most likely have legal right to buy her freedom. From a business perspective, the person with the favour is usually in the same field and understands the industry or power dynamics you are engaged in.

(ii) ***Secondly*** ***he is a man of great wealth-*** meaning that Boaz possessed the particular type of resources needed to address Naomi and Ruth's particular situation. From a business or leadership point of view, *great wealth* could refer to many things. For example, it may be a specific kind of information you need to boost your business' profitability or a strategy, technical equipment or human expertise or influence that the person of favour is already highly endowed with.

(iii) ***His name was Boaz*** – meaning that she had a timeframe within which her favour must be executed. In case you are wondering how that conclusion was reached, the name Boaz actually means "swiftness". Ruth, you will realize was a Moabite, a tribe avowed to be destroyed by Israel. In order for her to survive, she had to change her citizenship very swiftly through marriage to an Israelite.

(iv) ***"Please let me go to the field"*** – Ruth knew exactly where the favour was located and chose to go there. Interestingly, there is a chronological sense to all of this. If you do not know who your favour lies with, it is close to impossible to figure out its location. Many have misunderstood favour as being an intangible force that simply sweeps someone in its direction, but it is not so. The purpose of this book is not to change your perception on the subject but to provide another perspective that, hopefully, you can consider as real.

(v) ***"And glean heads of grain after him"*** – certainly she was to follow after him, not walk before him.

Ruth recognizes favour comes from one who has gone ahead of her and who has access to more leverage than she does. In the context of this book, this will equate to another business person or leader who has already gone ahead of you and who most likely has a greater leverage than you in the area in which you need the favour. If you are "ahead" of someone in a specific area, then you really cannot expect to seek favour from them in that particular field.

(vi) ***"In whose sight I may find favour"*** – and finally, Ruth teaches us about the need to position yourself in a way and in a place where favour can find you. The terminology *"in whose sight"* means there is need to position one's self in the path of vision of the other person from whom you are seeking favour – make yourself visible.

Principle 37

ORGANIZATIONAL PRIORITIES AND FAMILIARITY

1 Samuel 2: 27 – 36

[27] Then a man of God came to Eli and said to him, "Thus says the Lord: 'Did I not clearly reveal Myself to the house of your father when they were in Egypt in Pharaoh's house? [28] Did I not choose him out of all the tribes of Israel to be My priest, to offer upon My altar, to burn incense, and to wear an ephod before Me? And did I not give to the house of your father all the offerings of the children of Israel made by fire? [29] Why do you kick at My sacrifice and My offering which I have commanded in My dwelling place, and honour your sons more than Me, to make yourselves fat with the best of all the offerings of Israel My people?' [30] Therefore the Lord God of Israel says: 'I said indeed that your house and the house of your father would walk before Me forever.' But now the Lord says: 'Far be it from Me; for those who honour Me I will honour, and those who despise Me shall be lightly esteemed. [31] Behold, the days are coming that I will cut off your arm and the arm of your father's house, so that there will not be an old man in your house. [32] And you will see an

enemy in My dwelling place, despite all the good which God does for Israel. And there shall not be an old man in your house forever. [33] *But any of your men whom I do not cut off from My altar shall consume your eyes and grieve your heart. And all the descendants of your house shall die in the flower of their age.* [34] *Now this shall be a sign to you that will come upon your two sons, on Hophni and Phinehas: in one day they shall die, both of them.* [35] *Then I will raise up for Myself a faithful priest who shall do according to what is in My heart and in My mind. I will build him a sure house, and he shall walk before My anointed forever.* [36] *And it shall come to pass that everyone who is left in your house will come and bow down to him for a piece of silver and a morsel of bread, and say, "Please, put me in one of the priestly positions, that I may eat a piece of bread."*

The efficiency of your business operations or your leadership structure should never be compromised by familiarity. In the passage, God demonstrates to the Prophet Eli that not even the deepest form of familiarity - namely, blood relationships, should interfere with kingdom business. It should be so, for all forms of business and leadership.

You may have heard people say business and family do not mix. There's some degree of truth in it, but not in its entirety. Truth is, there have been some very successful family businesses and there will always be some degree of family involvement in business. What is NOT permissible however is for any such family relationship to rise above the overall interest of the business or institution.

People may argue that family relationships are more important than anything else and I will be equally quick to inform such persons that while this MAY be true, businesses, institutions and power structures, just like the family, also exist to serve God's purposes on earth. So let us look at some of the lessons emerging from the scripture.

Firstly, Eli and his sons were in the business of serving God's people, Israel. So here were a few people, serving a larger number – and that is typically the nature of businesses and institutions.

Secondly, Hophni and Phinehas, the sons of Eli were becoming a stumbling block to the thousands *Israelites* receiving services from the Temple. This can be equated to the employees of your company who are in the minority, becoming a hindrance in the service delivery to customers – the majority.

The struggle for Eli at this point was a hard one. His humanity and father's heart led him to defend his sons because they were his own blood – familiarity. But God wanted him to understand that when you are a leader, providing services to a larger number humanity, family relationship should never be allowed to compromise the greater good being done.

Do you realize that Eli, the chief executive, in protecting his two sons (employees), actually kept over three million Israelites from being blessed?

This is a hard thing for many to absorb and indeed it is worth giving some hope to the fainthearted. It is still possible and even useful in some cases, to do business or engage in leadership with family and other familiar persons. But you must ensure the lines are drawn from the start of such enterprise. It is also wise to review such arrangements from time to time to reflect changing circumstances.

Here is a final analogy to consider: Hophni and Phinehas were already serving the Lord before Samuel came along, so they both knew how to get the job done since they would have been well trained by Eli. It was hardly likely that Samuel knew any more than they did. The only difference seemed to be the fact that Samuel recognized the seriousness of the business of serving God's people and gave it the right attitude. That attitude was very different from his relationship with his own and Eli's family.

Principle 38

PRIORITISING ORGANISATIONAL STRUCTURES

2 Samuel 20:22 – 27

[22] Then the woman in her wisdom went to all the people. And they cut off the head of Sheba the son of Bichri, and threw it out to Joab. Then he blew a trumpet, and they withdrew from the city, every man to his tent. So Joab returned to the king at Jerusalem. [23] And Joab was over all the army of Israel; Benaiah the son of Jehoiada was over the Cherethites and the Pelethites; [24] Adoram was in charge of revenue; Jehoshaphat the son of Ahilud was recorder; [25] Sheva was scribe; Zadok and Abiathar were the priests; [26] and Ira the Jairite was a chief minister under David.

1 Kings 4: 1 – 7

So King Solomon was king over all Israel. [2] And these were his officials: Azariah the son of Zadok, the priest; [3] Elihoreph and Ahijah, the sons of Shisha, scribes; Jehoshaphat the son of Ahilud, the recorder; [4] Benaiah the son of Jehoiada, over the army; Zadok and Abiathar, the priests; [5] Azariah the son of Nathan, over the officers; Zabud the son of Nathan, a priest and the king's friend; [6] *Ahishar, over the household; and Adoniram the son of Abda, over the labour force.* [7] *And Solomon had twelve governors over all Israel, who provided food for the king and his household; each one made provision for one month of the year.*

Reading the passage from 2 Samuel, one can see how the hierarchy of David's governing body matched David's vision for Israel – he wanted to establish Israel as a supreme state militarily and politically. As a result of this vision, note the ranking of his officers in the passage above, in order of importance:

(i) The military or army commanders;
(ii) the chiefs of staff of political operations ;
(iii) the customs, revenue and taxation arm
(iv) the civil service
(v) administrators such as the scribes and
(vi) the priests

Looking at the top three ranks in David's government it is no surprise when biblical evidence reveals that he had Israel's strongest army, political order, and an excellent treasury department which ensured that most, if not all the nations conquered during war, paid taxes to him.

His son, Solomon, on the other hand, when he came into power had a different vision for Israel from his father. It was twofold. Solomon's first long term vision was to ensure the spiritual stability of Israel arising *from* his father David's final wish to build the holy temple for the LORD. Secondly, he was committed to education which can be deduced partly from the blessing of wisdom and understanding given him.

It is not surprising to observe the structure of Solomon's government in the passage from 1 Kings: There were

(i) priests
(ii) administrators (educational)
(iii) the civil service
(iv) the military
(v) more priests to reinforce his number one focus
(vi) secretaries of the state and
(vii) local governors.

In a quite fascinating twist, modern day Israel, has gone back to the order of David, and as a result, wield very strong military, intelligence and political power throughout the world.

Consider, however a country like Japan and China which over many years had focused on technology and are today's undisputed leaders in technology. I am not a human resource specialist, but since I learnt about these principles I am about to share with you now, my knowledge about recruitment of personnel has vastly changed.

Based on David and Solomon's organization of work-force, I have learned that some people or departments in your organisation must drive the vison whilst others must support drivers. In other words, where an organisation wants to be in the future should determine which department or people should be driving the organisation and which ones should be supporting it.

It does not mean that a given department will always be driving the organisation; rather, this should be determined by a leader who has the ability see into the future and where to position the organisation for optimal performance. Therefore, if the right team or unit drives the organisation, there is a greater possibility that the appointed vision will be achieved.

Recruitment should not be done based solely on the current needs of the organisation, but rather on the visualised future position of the company.

This wisdom does not only pertain to recruitment within an organisation, but also to you as an individual. Where you see yourself being in the future should determine how you prioritize your present activities and relationships.

Principle 39

ORGANISATIONAL FAILURES – THE SOURCE

Isaiah 39: 1 – 7

"At that time Merodach-Baladan the son of Baladan, king of Babylon, sent letters and a present to Hezekiah, for he heard that he had been sick and had recovered. And Hezekiah was pleased with them, and showed them the house of his treasures—the silver and gold, the spices and precious ointment, and all his armoury—all that was found among his treasures. There was nothing in his house or in all his dominion that Hezekiah did not show them. Then Isaiah the prophet went to King Hezekiah, and said to him, "What did these men say, and from where did they come to you?" So Hezekiah said, "They came to me from a far country, from Babylon." And he said, "What have they seen in your house?" So Hezekiah answered, "They have seen all that is in my house; there is nothing among my treasures that I have not shown them." Then Isaiah said to Hezekiah, "Hear the word of the Lord of hosts: 'Behold, the days are coming when all that is in your house, and what your fathers have accumulated until this day, shall be carried

to Babylon; nothing shall be left,' says the Lord. 'And they shall take away some of your sons who will descend from you, whom you will beget; and they shall be eunuchs in the palace of the king of Babylon.'"

There are many mistakes that can be made in business, leadership and politics and, most often, these are peculiar to the particular sector. In a very rare twist, the above passage highlights one cardinal sin which must never be committed whether in business, leadership or politics. Indeed it is grave enough to be classed a cardinal sin because permitting it to happen as the passage shows WILL most definitely:

1. Erase all your past achievements *("and all what your fathers have accumulated")*
2. Nullify all your present successes *("carry away all that is in your house")* and
3. Invalidate all your future potential accomplishments *("make your sons eunuchs")*

In other words, committing this cardinal sin has the potential to obliterate everything past, present and future with regard to your business operations, leadership prowess and political significance.

This cardinal sin is your failure to guard access to the secrets to your success or to carelessly divulge to outsiders *(Babylonians)*, knowledge about the three pillars upon which your business operations, leadership uniqueness or political strength are built. These pillars are:

1. Resources *(the gold and the silver)* – knowledge of your resources reveal your capabilities. It also gives insight into what you can acquire to boost your superiority.
2. Strategies Applied *(the ointment and spices)* – knowledge of your strategies tells the possessor of this kind of information where you will be, when you will be there and how you will even get there.
3. Defences *(the armoury)* – knowledge of your defences tells the recipient which of their attacks you can successfully withstand and those which you cannot.

For Hezekiah, and for anyone else, it does not matter whether the outsider is kind hearted or not, he is still a stranger. The term "outsider" does not only describe persons who are not members of your entity. In fact, every leader and political power broker must define for themselves who falls within this category of "outsider"; furthermore, having a kind heart does not exempt anyone from being classified as an outsider.

The hard truth to accept is that people are generally kind-hearted until they have access to what it takes to change their hearts and, from that point on, it all depends on how much of God they have allowed into themselves. This you can never know until it is too late.

Principle 40

MAKING LASTING CHOICES & DECISIONS

Genesis 21: 8 – 16

So the child grew and was weaned. And Abraham made a great feast on the same day that Isaac was weaned. And Sarah saw the son of Hagar the Egyptian, whom she had borne to Abraham, scoffing. Therefore she said to Abraham, "Cast out this bondwoman and her son; for the son of this bondwoman shall not be heir with my son, namely with Isaac." And the matter was very displeasing in Abraham's sight because of his son. But God said to Abraham, "Do not let it be displeasing in your sight because of the lad or because of your bondwoman. Whatever Sarah has said to you, listen to her voice; for in Isaac your seed shall be called. Yet I will also make a nation of the son of the bondwoman, because he is your seed." So Abraham rose early in the morning, and took bread and a skin of water; and putting it on her shoulder, he gave it and the boy to Hagar, and sent her away. Then she departed and wandered in the Wilderness of Beersheba. And the water in the skin was used up, and she placed the boy under one of the shrubs.

Then she went and sat down across from him at a distance of about a bowshot; for she said to herself, "Let me not see the death of the boy." So she sat opposite him, and lifted her voice and wept.

Here is a fascinating story about Abraham, as CEO of his home, caught in-between Hagar and Sarah. This is an excellent example of conflict resolution, decision-making and discipline, all of which are likely to arise in every business, social, religious or political organisation.

Let's analyse the situation outlined in the passage. Abraham had been intimate with both women, knew both well and their degrees of loyalty to him. The two sons were his seed, having come from his loins. So what is the criterion with which to determine banishing one son into the wilderness and the other to remain with him?

To find the answer, you will need to ask another question: *"which of the choices, if followed, will draw him closer to God?"* Isaac was the child of promise and the seed of covenant, destiny and prophecy, while Ishmael was not. Sarah, Isaac's mother was a covenant wife of Abraham; Hagar was not.

In leadership of any kind, choices will daily have to be made between two cherished ideas or two well liked employees or feasible prospects.

The lesson here is that where you have to make a decision between two or more seemingly equally balanced choices, always settle for the option that moves you closer to conforming to God's purposes received in the form of a covenant, a vow, a prophesy or other.

Principle 41

HOW TO HANDLE VITAL INFORMATION

1 Samuel 10: 14 – 16

"Then Saul's uncle said to him and his servant, "Where did you go?" So he said, "To look for the donkeys. When we saw that they were nowhere to be found, we went to Samuel." And Saul's uncle said, "Tell me, please, what Samuel said to you." So Saul said to his uncle, "He told us plainly that the donkeys had been found." But about the matter of the kingdom, he did not tell him what Samuel had said."

Judges 16: 13 – 18

"Delilah said to Samson, "Until now you have mocked me and told me lies. Tell me what you may be bound with." And he said to her, "If you weave the seven locks of my head into the web of the loom"— so she wove it tightly with the batten of the loom, and said to him, "The Philistines are upon you, Samson!" But he awoke from his sleep, and pulled out the batten and the web from the loom. Then she said to him, "How can you say, 'I love you,' when your heart is not with me? You have mocked me these three times, and

have not told me where your great strength lies." And it came to pass, when she pestered him daily with her words and pressed him, so that his soul was vexed to death, that he told her all his heart, and said to her, "No razor has ever come upon my head, for I have been a Nazirite to God from my mother's womb. If I am shaven, then my strength will leave me, and I shall become weak, and be like any other man." When Delilah saw that he had told her all his heart, she sent and called for the lords of the Philistines, saying, "Come up once more, for he has told me all his heart." So the lords of the Philistines came up to her and brought the money in their hand."

As a business person, leader, or a politician, one of the hard and fast rules to live by is to always exercise discretion with vital information.

In the two passages we see how Saul and Samson deal with vital information. Samson, despite his great strength, divulged vital information to the wrong person, and it cost him everything. Saul on the other hand, understood this very crucial principle that *not everybody needs to know everything.*

You must understand that at all times you are trading information – but in this kind of trade, the utmost priority is not so much the price at which you sell the information or the profit made from it, but with whom and when you trade the information. I strongly deduced that if Saul had disclosed the information about his emerging kingship to his uncle, he very likely would never have become king.

I cannot stress enough the dire importance of not saying everything to everybody. I'll attempt to list below a few circumstances in which you must not divulge part or all the information you have:

1. If the information holds the key to your strength or your weakness and the person seeking it has had or still has some allegiance or connection to past or current enemies, no matter how remote, as happened in the case of Samson and Delilah.

2. If the information disclosed now might jeopardise success in the future and especially if it is being requested very close to an impending promotion as in the case of Saul's uncle wanting to know all that Samuel had said to him.

3. If the information is likely to bring harm to the one receiving it *(as in the case of Absalom, the son of David and Ahithophel).* This requires a good knowledge of the weaknesses of the one receiving the information. One needs

to understand that some people may require information but it may harm them because they are not ready to handle it properly.

4. If the recipient of the information is already seeking to gain the same advantage as you, even without such information as with Haaman and Mordecai in the book of Esther.

5. If the recipient of the information already hates you or is not entirely favourable towards you. We see this with Joseph and his brothers. The Bible tells us in Genesis 37:5 that after he shared the dream, they hated him "even more," presupposing that they already hated him even before he told them the dream.

6. If the appropriate time of releasing the information does not align with when it is being requested. It is worth understanding that not all information should be made accessible at all times. Some kinds of information are best deployed at their appropriate time. Habakkuk 2:3 says: *"For the vision is yet <u>for an appointed time</u>; but at the end it will speak, and it will not lie. Though it tarries, wait for it; because it will surely come, it will not tarry."*

Principle 42

ASSUMPTIONS – THE MOTHER OF ALL FAILURES

1 Samuel 17: 23 – 27

Then as he talked with them, there was the champion, the Philistine of Gath, Goliath by name, coming up from the armies of the Philistines; and he spoke according to the same words. So David heard them. And all the men of Israel, when they saw the man, fled from him and were dreadfully afraid. So the men of Israel said, "Have you seen this man who has come up? Surely he has come up to defy Israel; and it shall be that the man who kills him the king will enrich with great riches, will give him his daughter, and give his father's house exemption from taxes in Israel." Then David spoke to the men who stood by him, saying, "What shall be done for the man who kills this Philistine and takes away the reproach from Israel? For who is this uncircumcised Philistine, that he should defy the armies of the living God?" And the people answered him in this manner, saying, "So shall it be done for the man who kills him."

Genesis 18: 21

I will go down now and see whether they have done altogether according to the outcry against it that has come to Me; and if not, I will know.”

If there is one thing you learn from this book, let it be the fact that if you wish to succeed as a business person, a leader or a politician or at anything that you do, you should never assume anything. Assumption is the mother of all failures and the father of all regrets.

Indeed, assumption is the womb in which every lost opportunity is grown. You only have to thoroughly trace the root cause of any form of failure and you are likely to discover that there was some false assumption made along the way. Unfortunately most times, such wrong assumptions could have been avoided.

In the passage from 1st Samuel – David saw an opportunity, but he made the wise decision of not assuming what the outcomes from such an opportunity would be, so he applied the dual test which is to test if the assumption will apply in two opposite scenarios.

You see, when David first heard about the possible *rewards (a princess for a wife, riches and tax exemptions)* for killing Goliath, the men from whom he heard it, were running from the Goliath in fear. In that state, David understood that humans are likely to say and promise anything in order to escape that which they dreaded, so he could not safely assume what the men of Israel told him was absolutely true.

Others would have straightaway believed the men because they fellow Israelites and some, his own brothers. Indeed, they were all people with whom he was closely connected. But David knew better than to act on assumption in making such huge commitment to face Goliath.

Therefore, in verse 26 of the same text, David now consciously asks the men to confirm what he had previously heard. They repeated the same rewards for anyone killing Goliath. The big difference this time was that the men were not running, but rather "standing" – indicative of them being of sound mind and reasoning.

Let me emphasis even further the importance of subjecting every assumption to the dual test before making any decision. If you have ever had any such experience, you will know that more often than not, what you hear from people when they offer you information is different from what you hear from the same people when you request the same information.

The difference is that in the first scenario, they are the initiators and as such are likely to control and determine the scope and parameters of the information they offer you, while in the latter instance, you do. I have found that where information obtained unsolicited matches that received based upon request, then that information is more likely to be correct. If by any chance the two conflict, even in the slightest way, you should use that information cautiously or not at all. When David first heard about the opportunities, it was told to him, but in verse 26, he asked for it.

I guess I should say I am out to prove how very important this principle is to your success in business, leadership and political power. It is so significant that even God uses it. That's right! He does, so never assumes anything and if you must, then put your assumption through the *duality* test.

In the second text from Genesis, thousands and perhaps millions of complaints were made to God about the sinful ways of Sodom and Gomorrah. In our humanness alone, a very reasonable assumption we would have made would be – *"all these millions of people, saying the same thing against one little town cannot all be wrong"*.

But what does God Himself do? He comes down to see for Himself and by that, the requirements of the duality test, that is, hearing it unsolicited first, then seeing it for Himself afterwards was confirmed. Only then did He send down the destruction.

Just like David's, the first set of information in the form of complaints came up to God unsolicited. He did not ask for it, but when He came down to see, it was Him putting in His own effort to find an objective answer. In short, it was Him asking, not passively receiving it.

Finally, another important area not to assume anything is – whether your employees, customers and stakeholders know what you think they ought to know.

Never assume your followers know. The only valid assumption to ever make is that nobody knows unless you tell them. To borrow one of the rules of the US's Federal Bureau of Investigation *(FBI)*, *"what you see and what you hear are not always what they seem to be"*, and by extension "what people see and what they hear about you are never what it seems to be."

Remember, do not ever make any assumptions. All failures in business, leadership and politics are fathered by it. If out of necessity you must make an assumption, always make sure it passes the duality test.

Principle 43

TIMING OF PUBLIC EXPOSURES

Mathew 2: 1 – 4, 7 – 8, 16

"Now after Jesus was born in Bethlehem of Judea in the days of Herod the king, behold, wise men from the East came to Jerusalem, saying, 'Where is He who has been born King of the Jews? For we have seen His star in the East and have come to worship Him.' When Herod the king heard this, he was troubled, and all Jerusalem with him. And when he had gathered all the chief priests and scribes of the people together, he inquired of them where the Christ was to be born."

"Then Herod, when he had secretly called the wise men, determined from them what time the star appeared. And he sent them to Bethlehem and said, "Go and search carefully for the young Child, and when you have found Him, bring back word to me, that I may come and worship Him also."

"Then Herod, when he saw that he was deceived by the wise men, was exceedingly angry; and he sent forth and put to

death all the male children who were in Bethlehem and in all its districts, from two years old and under, according to the time which he had determined from the wise men"

In the above scripture, Jesus is born and His arrival is soon advertised by the stars, the three wise men and Herod's philosophers. Right after the advertisements, King Herod sanctions a massacre, targeting every male child in order to get to baby Jesus.

As remote as this biblical story may appear from modern day business, leadership and politics, it nevertheless has an important lesson to teach us. We learn that the arrival of a new thing does not necessarily warrant its publicity. This is certainly a good lesson to remember in your quest for a successful leadership.

The fact that you have new knowledge, a new idea or product with the potential of making a huge profit does not necessarily mean it has to be publicized. It really is all about timing. Joseph, in the book of Genesis, faced a similar problem in telling his brothers about his dreams of dominion over them which the Bible says made them *"hate him even more."* Indeed, his untimely announcement marked the beginning of his castigation. I am of the belief that Joseph would still have become prime minister of Egypt without having to go through all the troubles of being cast into the pit, sold into slavery and thrown in jail.

A great deal of business, power and leadership success depends on your ability to time when and to whom new information is made available. In fact, sometimes, the sudden arrival of a new thing does not even require that the information goes out about its arrival and potential use.

King Herod can symbolize another existing project or product, a rival idea, or your known competitors. That means basically anyone or anything whose potential importance or relevance to you is likely to diminish as a result of the unfolding of your new knowledge. This perception could turn them against you.

Wisdom demands that you know when to determine the right time to unfold certain knowledge.

Principle 44

CRITERIA FOR MAKING LONG LASTING DECISIONS

Mathew 4: 1 – 4

Then Jesus was led up by the Spirit into the wilderness to be tempted by the devil. And when He had fasted forty days and forty nights, afterward He was hungry. Now when the tempter came to Him, he said, "If You are the Son of God, command that these stones become bread." But He answered and said, "It is written, 'Man shall not live by bread alone, but by every word that proceeds from the mouth of God.'"

Jesus was hungry after a long fast, so satan asked Him to turn stones to bread and eat it. Jesus had a need for food and He also needed to make a decision. What satan did was simply to give Jesus a choice. In actual fact, satan acknowledged something very profound that most of us Christians gloss over when reading this passage. By asking Jesus to turn stones into bread, he was more or less acknowledging that only He had what it took to turn impossibilities into possibilities.

But here is an even more crucial lesson we should learn

from the passage – every leadership decision you will ever make results from a need. It does not matter whether it is an immediate, future or past need.

As a Christian leader, it is worth understanding a few things: Firstly, Jesus did not refuse to turn the stones into bread because he could not; after all He later proved His miracle working credentials by turning water into wine. Rather, He was trying to teach two very fundamental leadership lessons:

1. Every successful decision must be able to produce a solution for the current need and
2. Provide a solution beyond the current need.

It must be able to answer positively to the question - *"will the outcome of this decision establish a sustainable solution beyond the present need?"* If you apply this criterion in your decision-making, you will be able to judge whether any decision you are about to make will be successful or not – even before you make it.

Jesus could have easily turned stones into bread, but it would have only satisfied His current hunger and not the future ones because bread DOES RUN OUT. Instead, he deploys the Word of God, the working of which provides bread for the body, spirit and soul for eternity. That's successful decision – sustained solutions beyond the present need.

Principle 45

EXERCISING POWER OVER COMPETITORS

1 Samuel 17: 45 – 47

"Then David said to the Philistine, "You come to me with a sword, with a spear, and with a javelin. But I come to you in the name of the Lord of hosts, the God of the armies of Israel, whom you have defied. This day the Lord will deliver you into my hand, and I will strike you and take your head from you. And this day I will give the carcasses of the camp of the Philistines to the birds of the air and the wild beasts of the earth, that all the earth may know that there is a God in Israel. Then all this assembly shall know that the Lord does not save with sword and spear; for the battle is the Lord's, and He will give you into our hands."

In this passage are a number of lessons which cannot be contained in these few paragraphs. However, I will try to highlight one that I think is key to successful leadership.

Hidden in this text is a tool, which if properly applied will ALWAYS make you appear very powerful, give you leverage and make you revered whether in leadership, in business or in power.

Unknown to a lot of people, David actually won the battle with Goliath before he even put a stone in his sling. How did he do it? He weakened Goliath and left him utterly exposed - spirit, soul and body. David applied a two-pronged strategy that is still being used by business, political and military leaders to exercise influential leverage over others. And here it is in very plain English: *the art of making your opponent appear known and exposed and you invisible*".

By telling Goliath "you come to me with your sword, spear and javelin but I come in the name of the LORD the God of Host", David was saying more than what you just read and, most certainly, it was having a greater impact on Goliath than many have imagined until now. Essentially, David was making Goliath aware that his *(Goliath's)* weapons, how they are operated and their individual capabilities were known and as such, provision could be made for protection against them – they were visible.

On the other hand, David's weapon (i.e. God and His Host) was not known to Goliath, neither were they visible, so could not be defended against.

Now, ask yourself, how you would feel if you walked into a battle and realised that you had no knowledge whatsoever of the weapons your opponent was going to use because they were invisible. Right there you realise that if you did not know these two variables, you could neither attack him nor defend yourself against him. It is more than likely that you would be petrified easily prone to defeated.

Four of the surest ways to achieve this in business, politics and leadership are:

(i) as much as possible, even if pushed to the wall, be exceptionally sparse with words or to add a twist, say nothing when everyone expects you to speak and say little when no one expects you to talk at all
(ii) Make yourself unknown – do not make yourself overly available and predictable in people's eye
(iii) every time you meet with your opponents, critics or doubters, make obvious what you know about them that they would not have imagined you knew and
(iv) always withhold and control information about yourself and your next move.

At the time of writing this book, three of the most powerful leaders in the world are Angela Merkel, the German Chancellor, Vladimir Putin, the Russian president and the Rothschild family, easily the world's Richest family. Whereas Ms Merkel has very well applied (i) and (ii), Putin has always applied (i), (iii) and (iv) whereas, the Rothschild family, who is still largely unknown to many as one of the world's richest families has effectively deployed (i) and (iv).

In one sentence: make everybody else seem exposed and yourself, cryptic. The truth is, the less people know about your real strength and your moves, the more powerful you appear and the more you know about theirs the more vulnerable they appear to you. A combination of the two is a guaranteed strategy for winning.

Principle 46

HOW TO CREATE INFLUENCE OVER OTHERS

Mathew 9: 1 – 8

"So He got into a boat, crossed over, and came to His own city. Then behold, they brought to Him a paralytic lying on a bed. When Jesus saw their faith, He said to the paralytic, 'Son, be of good cheer; your sins are forgiven you.' And at once some of the scribes said within themselves, 'this Man blasphemes!' But Jesus, knowing their thoughts, said, 'Why do you think evil in your hearts? For which is easier, to say, your sins are forgiven you, or to say, arise and walk? But that you may know that the Son of Man has power on earth to forgive sins'—then He said to the paralytic, 'Arise, take up your bed, and go to your house.' And he arose and departed to his house. Now when the multitudes saw it, they marvelled and glorified God, who had given such power to men."

Power does not necessarily come from violence, but if you know what to do, power is achievable without the usual connotations of evil and wickedness.

In fact Jesus in His time, wielded power – power with which to do good. It will interest many to know that it was not just spiritual power, he wielded world power too. If your business, your leadership and your political presence is going to make any impact, then you must be known, you must be heard, people must be eager to want to know what you are doing or will be doing. In short, people must be willing to settle their doubts on certain issues by hearing your position. It's called having *"good influence."* Here, Jesus teaches us two of the core ingredients to acquiring influence.

From the passage, there are two ways Jesus could have healed the paralytic and He was capable of using both methods. The one was to heal him the orthodox way (take him to the physicians), which is what the Jews expected from Him, and the other was to use the less known, unorthodox way (heal him by nothing other than his word). He chose the latter NOT because He could not apply the former; but using the latter gave Him influence over the Jews and all the people, because *they knew of no such method and yet it yielded a much better and faster result.*

There is one thing worth knowing about human nature and which you might have been taught in economics and it is that *human beings are insatiable.* Subconsciously, we are always excited about a new way of doing things and we tend to place great value on people who create new and exciting things. You can therefore imagine the reception Jesus would have received in being the first man to have unorthodoxly healed another by simply forgiving him of his sins. Apart from the novelty of this, the result would have been much more startling since it was instantaneous, permanent and infinitely better than the widely accepted physician approach.

So there you have it- the key to creating influence is to be unorthodox in your approach:

1. Use an unorthodox approach to providing a solution if it is at all possible and especially, if it has never been used before.
2. Make sure the results are bigger and better than what the outcome of a traditional approach would have yielded.
3. Make sure you are equally capable of employing the traditional approach. Any argument that you only used the unorthodox approach because you are incapable of using the traditional method will weaken the impact of your unorthodox approach.

I have realized many Christians do not truly appreciate the need to be influential because they associate this with being "worldly". While this book does not deal with such a perspective on influence, it is worth stating that influence is both a powerful tool in evangelism and for countering wickedness in the world. If you have ever had any experience evangelising you will understand how difficult it can be to get an unbeliever to even want to listen to you, let alone being willing to hear about Jesus. Now consider how that would be different, if as a result of your positive *influence*, many are already eager to hear what you have to say.

Principle 47

THE VALUE OF "PEOPLE" IN THE SUCCESS EQUATION

Mathew 9: 9 – 10

"As Jesus passed on from there, He saw a man named Matthew sitting at the tax office. And He said to him, 'Follow Me.' So he arose and followed Him. Now it happened, as Jesus sat at the table in the house, that behold, many tax collectors and sinners came and sat down with Him and His disciples."

Ecclesiastes 10:19

"A feast is made for laughter, And wine makes merry; But money answers everything."

Genesis 7:14

"They and every beast after its kind, all cattle after their kind, every creeping thing that creeps on the earth after its kind, and every bird after its kind, every bird of every sort."

Money, they say, makes the world go round. Indeed, the Bible does say it answers to everything. Whatever your ideas, plans or strategies, without money and people, they will not happen.

Without these two vital ingredients, your plans will remain exactly where they originated – in your mind and heart – and will never be manifested or become a reality. But here are two useful things I wish to say about this that you should hold on to:

(i) Money NEVER grows on trees – it lives in the hands and pockets of "PEOPLE", so if you have any intention of being wealthy, you need to start connecting with people and attracting them into your life. You will need others to help you find where wealth is located, to dig it out of a known location and to maintain it after it has been dug out. "*I am naturally not a people person*" is no longer a valid excuse from the very day God said: "*it is not good for man to be alone.*"

(ii) Taxation is the only combined Godly and legal way by which money, which is rightfully yours can be lost or maintained. I can understand that you have read many books on wealth creation and the seven steps to make wealth, but here is what they do not tell you – making money is the easy part. Keeping it is the real challenge. If you care to know a secret, it is this – the rich always make good friends with the taxman.

In the passage from Mathew above, Jesus by His action teaches us two very practical and useful lessons:

1. When you set up a business, you did so to satisfy the needs of people. When you went into leadership and politics, you would have realised that without a following of people you would neither be a leader nor a politician. But in your own *circles of influence (i.e. those who immediately influence you and strategically support your success and vision)* you must consciously determine who is a part of your inner circle and those who are not. In other words, you must distinguish between the people whom you impact, but over whom you do not have too much control, and those who influence, support and push your vision and dreams. The latter are the ones you must have a control over in terms who you accept onto that team.

   In the passage above we learn that if you draw farmers into your circle of influence, do not automatically expect to be seated at a table full of accountants, lawyers and government officials. The secret is shown in *Genesis 7:14 – everything follows after their kind.*

Jesus invited one tax collector by the name of Mathew to follow him, by evening, many tax collectors had gathered to Him. He invited four fishermen as his first disciples and the next thing was the whole fishing community of Galilee had gathered to Him. It is NOT mere coincidence – *everything follows after its kind.*

2. The second lesson is this – no matter who you have in your circle of influence, make sure they include tax men. As a business person, taxes if planned well or unplanned, can make or break your profitability. As a leader, understand that taxation is one single element that can wipe away the earnings of those you are leading. As a politician, understand that the issue of tax will be on the agenda for the rest of your life and winning the debate on the issue is winning with many people – because it affects everybody.

Principle 48

HANDLING ALLEGATIONS AND DOUBTS

Mathew 11: 1 – 8

Now it came to pass, when Jesus finished commanding His twelve disciples that He departed from there to teach and to preach in their cities. And when John had heard in prison about the works of Christ, he sent two of[a] his disciples and said to Him, "Are You the Coming One, or do we look for another?" Jesus answered and said to them, "Go and tell John the things which you hear and see: the blind see and the lame walk; the lepers are cleansed and the deaf hear; the dead are raised up and the poor have the gospel preached to them. 6 And blessed is he who is not offended because of Me." As they departed, Jesus began to say to the multitudes concerning John: "What did you go out into the wilderness to see? A reed shaken by the wind? But what did you go out to see? A man clothed in soft garments? Indeed, those who wear soft clothing are in kings' houses.

As a leader and a politician of a Godly order, you ought to understand that your methods, principles, ideologies and concepts may often times be questioned or challenged.

This happens because they are radically different from those of the world system. You are very likely to be faced with a constant need to justify your approach.

What you don't want happening however, is the scenario where your justifications end up scattering your customers or your supporters. In the text above, Jesus, the master businessman and leader shows us how to prevent this from happening:

1. Do not ever make the error of explaining yourself or trying to justify your actions. Whatever you do, avoid doing this or else you will only end up giving your opponents more weapons with which to fight you. This is exactly the position they want you in – to give them a long enough rope with which to lower you deeper into a well. When you get into the position of attempting to justify yourself beyond a reasonable explanation, you will surely start saying more than you need to and so could inadvertently provide more information usable against you.

2. Refer those who are requiring the explanations to undeniable evidence, testimonials and proofs. This kind of evidence is a very powerful tool and, for the most part, can be very effective in removing any element of doubt. Proof, evidence and testimonials that are available for all to see serve as a common measure everybody *(including your opponents)* can see. This should silence the doubts and help dismiss the allegations.

By doing these two things, you will be providing a self-sustaining mechanism by which future allegations and doubts will be handled without your necessary involvement. A further piece of advice is to always make sure you have a catalogue of positive evidence about the impact your operations are making on its target group.

Document as much as you practically can because you will most certainly need such records someday.

Principle 49

A WARFARE STRATEGY AGAINST COMPETITORS

Mathew 12: 22 – 30

Then one was brought to Him who was demon-possessed, blind and mute; and He healed him, so that the blind and[a] mute man both spoke and saw. 23 And all the multitudes were amazed and said, "Could this be the Son of David?" Now when the Pharisees heard it they said, "This fellow does not cast out demons except by Beelzebub, the ruler of the demons." But Jesus knew their thoughts, and said to them: "Every kingdom divided against itself is brought to desolation, and every city or house divided against itself will not stand. If Satan casts out Satan, he is divided against himself. How then will his kingdom stand? And if I cast out demons by Beelzebub, by whom do your sons cast them out? Therefore they shall be your judges. But if I cast out demons by the Spirit of God, surely the kingdom of God has come upon you. Or how can one enter a strong man's house and plunder his goods, unless he first binds the strong man? And then he will plunder his house. He who is not with Me is against Me, and he who does not gather with Me scatters abroad

Acts 23: 6 – 9

"But when Paul perceived that one part were Sadducees and the other Pharisees, he cried out in the council, 'Men and brethren, I am a Pharisee, the son of a Pharisee; concerning the hope and resurrection of the dead I am being judged!' And when he had said this, a dissension arose between the Pharisees and the Sadducees; and the assembly was divided. For Sadducees say that there is no resurrection—and no angel or spirit; but the Pharisees confess both. Then there arose a loud outcry. And the scribes of the Pharisees' party arose and protested, saying, "We find no evil in this man; but if a spirit or an angel has spoken to him, let us not fight against God."

This is one of those rare lessons from the Bible that I am very careful sharing because it has the nature of a double-edged sword. It can be used to defend as well as to destroy. It is my Godly expectation of those reading it, that it will not be used indiscriminately for the unwarranted destruction of others.

Many times I have always thought of this passage as merely a teaching on the kingdom of satan and that of God, until God revealed its hidden usefulness in business, leadership and politics. Again, I repeat, it is not being shown here for a destructive purpose but primarily for you to know it is a method that can be used against you, and if this happens, that you will have a fair idea how to counter it.

No army fights and wins when it is divided. This is not the same as a single army in different locations. In other words, I am saying you can have all the members of one army located in one place but divided among themselves on various issues. If you have ever been in the military, you will know that no platoon is sent out if there are serious disagreements among its members because these are likely to produce mental, ideological or psychological fragmentations. On the other hand also, you could have another platoon dispersed to different locations yet its members are still united mentally, ideologically and psychologically.

Disunity among team members is like a time bomb waiting to implode. Creating internal dissention or confusion has the effect of using up all of an organisation's energy to maintain the strife as well as to resolve it. Consequently, there is little or no energy left to fight the external enemy.

It is a deadly strategy, which if deployed appropriately against your competitors, has the added advantage of using their own resources to weaken them from within.

This is what Jesus meant when He indicated that a kingdom divided against itself cannot stand. It takes energy to stand; and if that energy is being used to diffuse internal dissentions, there will be none left for standing against an external attack, hence the imminent defeat.

There are practically two ways of achieving this implosive result and one of them is used by the apostle Paul in Acts 23. All you have to do is to locate an area of dissension within your target organisation. This could relate to a philosophy, methodology, product, policy or an important controversial decision. Then all you have to do is to set any of these areas ablaze in a way that triggers an explosive disagreement and the implosion is bound to follow.

This having been said, I want you to appreciate that in the case of apostle, Paul, he did not use it indiscriminately, but only resorted to this method when he realised that the mixed council of Sadducees and Pharisees had wilfully gathered against him to bring about his death. By employing this strategy, Paul escaped an untimely death that would have prevented him from writing most of the New Testament and carrying the gospel message to thousands of people all over the world.

The second approach is to immobilize the strongman of your target organisation. By this I do not mean doing anything that is harmful to the individual. The strongman of a target organisation may not even be a person, instead it could be a successful working philosophy, a system or the rival organisation's core product or how its service is delivered. For the politician, it could be the leadership style or a political ideology that is popular with the masses.

For this reason, it is of vital importance to find out who or what is the real strong man of the organisation, otherwise, you may be binding the wrong thing or person. Binding the strong man is about doing anything to GENUINELY discredit the strongman's established potency.

Whatever it is, it must first and foremost be genuine, if it is merely a smear campaign it will not work, and *"assuming"* that it is genuine will not make it genuine either.

Principle 50

PREPARING FOR BUSINESS OPPORTUNITIES

Mathew 25: 1 – 13

*Then the kingdom of heaven shall be likened to ten virgins
who took their lamps and went out to meet the bridegroom. 2 Now five of them were wise, and five were foolish.
3 Those who were foolish took their lamps and took no oil
with them, 4 but the wise took oil in their vessels with their
lamps. 5 But while the bridegroom was delayed, they all
slumbered and slept. 6 "And at midnight a cry was heard:
'Behold, the bridegroom is coming; go out to meet him!' 7
Then all those virgins arose and trimmed their lamps. 8 And
the foolish said to the wise, 'Give us some of your oil, for
our lamps are going out.' 9 But the wise answered, saying,
'No, lest there should not be enough for us and you; but
go rather to those who sell, and buy for yourselves.' 10 And
while they went to buy, the bridegroom came, and those
who were ready went in with him to the wedding; and the
door was shut. 11 "Afterward the other virgins came also,
saying, 'Lord, Lord, open to us!' 12 But he answered and
said, 'Assuredly, I say to you, I do not know you.' 13 "Watch*

therefore, for you know neither the day nor the hour in which the Son of Man is coming

This is one of those few passages that directly relates to business and enterprise than it does to leadership, although I must honestly assert that there are very valuable general lessons other leaders can learn from it. In order to proceed, I will break down each verse and the valuable lessons it teaches:

1. *Verse 1:* Generally, a virgin is any woman who has not known a man intimately. In business, where no one knows the future they can be considered as virgins. This lack of knowledge does not discount the fact God can reveal the future to you if He so chooses, but that's entirely up to His sovereignty. It neither means your ignorance about the future should prevent you from expecting major opportunity. This expected opportunity is represented by the awaited groom. Frankly, if you go into businesses not expecting future opportunities, then you shouldn't be in business in the first place.

2. *Verses 2 – 6*: Taking a group of virgin business people (with equally no knowledge about the future), the criteria to determine those that end up successful and those that don't, lies in whether they are wise or foolish virgins. In similar fashion, there are only two types of business people – the wise and the foolish. Understand, however, that being wise or foolish in business has absolutely nothing to do with the volume or quality of information you have, but rather with how well you prepare for the unknown future. The "oil" is the *prior preparation* that sustains you *(lamp still burning)* beyond the point of meeting your opportunity *(the groom).*

Regarding the foolish virgins, *(and do feel the freedom to extend this to a business scenario)*, it must have been heart-breaking to have preserved themselves for so long, journeyed so far with lamp in hand and heard about the arrival of their perfect groom – and yet could not have their fill of love because their rooms had suddenly gone dark.

In the darkness, neither they nor the groom could find each other. Suffice it to say, the groom would not be waiting in that darkness for long because there were other virgin brides with lights in their rooms.

Now is a perfect time to highlight these few truths: (i) the future will always come bringing in it opportunities

(ii) when the specific future time comes, in which is hidden specific opportunities and they are not seized, those opportunities will fly away – just like time flies away.

3. Verses 7 – 10: Some Christians have the unusual belief that they must say "yes" to every request made to them. I have never quite understood the phenomenon. However, I must say that in business there are times when you need to say no if you want to be consistently successful in the future. You should never share the preparedness you have consciously made to grasp certain opportunities when they present themselves, just as how the wise virgins refused to share their oil with the foolish ones.

   In refusing to share your information about your preparation, you should not feel for a moment that you are sinning. Your ability to make the most of an opportunity comes from the amount of oil you acquired before the groom's arrival. Being prepared will determine how well you enjoy the business opportunities that arise in the future.

4. Lastly, the core message in this entire passage is – being prepared to take advantage of opportunities that arise any time in the future. The groom could have arrived just when the virgins started the journey or after a month or

year. The certainty for them was that the groom would come. This is the same with opportunities – you're never sure of its time of arrival, but it comes.

Your oil *(preparation)*, which enables you to make the best "use" of the groom *(opportunities)* when he arrives, could be one of many things. For a business, it could be:

(i) the liquid cash you keep aside to take advantage of once in a lifetime investment opportunities that may never come again;

(ii) the organisation's operational structures you have put in place to take advantage of sudden opportunities to expand in your industry or;

(iii) a development of your staff's ability to quickly adapt to change which will allow them to recognize and embrace new opportunities faster when they arise. In fact, without even knowing that they are operating according to biblical principles, many successful organisations in the secular world are seeing the benefits of training their staff to become more multi-faceted, so they can quickly adapt to change.

Principle 51

REPLICATING LEADERSHIP SUCCESSES

Mathew 25: 14 – 30

14 “For the kingdom of heaven is like a man traveling to a far country, who called his own servants and delivered his goods to them. 15 And to one he gave five talents, to another two, and to another one, to each according to his own ability; and immediately he went on a journey. 16 Then he who had received the five talents went and traded with them, and made another five talents. 17 And likewise he who had received two gained two more also. 18 But he who had received one went and dug in the ground, and hid his lord’s money. 19 After a long time the lord of those servants came and settled accounts with them. 20 “So he who had received five talents came and brought five other talents, saying, ‘Lord, you delivered to me five talents; look, I have gained five more talents besides them.’ 21 His lord said to him, ‘Well done, good and faithful servant; you were faithful over a few things, I will make you ruler over many things. Enter into the joy of your lord.’ 22 He also who had received two talents came and said, ‘Lord, you delivered to me two talents; look,

I have gained two more talents besides them.' [23] *His lord said to him, 'Well done, good and faithful servant; you have been faithful over a few things, I will make you ruler over many things. Enter into the joy of your lord.'* [24] *"Then he who had received the one talent came and said, 'Lord, I knew you to be a hard man, reaping where you have not sown, and gathering where you have not scattered seed.* [25] *And I was afraid, and went and hid your talent in the ground. Look, there you have what is yours.'* [26] *"But his lord answered and said to him, 'You wicked and lazy servant, you knew that I reap where I have not sown, and gather where I have not scattered seed.* [27] *So you ought to have deposited my money with the bankers, and at my coming I would have received back my own with interest.* [28] *Therefore take the talent from him, and give it to him who has ten talents.* [29] *'For to everyone who has, more will be given, and he will have abundance; but from him who does not have, even what he has will be taken away.* [30] *And cast the unprofitable servant into the outer darkness. There will be weeping and gnashing of teeth.'*

I enjoy having the opportunity of commenting on one of the most popular parables of the Bible. Over the years this parable of the ten talents has mainly been used to teach us about the need to use our individual talents effectively for God. However, you will be surprised to know it also presents a very important lesson on leadership at all levels.

Let's bear in mind that one can only be a leader because others choose to follow and the quality of one's leadership will always be measured by the impact made on those led. For Jesus, His target was to die on the cross to make salvation available to all and in the process, successfully impacted the lives of twelve disciples He was leading.

In the parable narrated above, we could quite comfortably say the man who gave out the talents was successful as both a businessman and a leader because: (i) he succeeded in multiplying his wealth overall which is the number one target of every business person (ii) he provided the resources which enabled his servants to trade. This is interesting because they were simply servants, and had it not been for the businessman's foresight, they would never have had discovered their own trading potentials.

Another interesting leadership revelation to be gleaned from this parable is that one of the easiest, surest, most effective ways of consistently achieving more results is to duplicate your abilities and talents. Here is something to consider – the talents were never for the servants, all along they belonged to the master UNTIL he gave it out. Yes, he had done all the trading with the talents previously without involving his servants, until he took the risk of training and entrusting them with HIS talents.

The idea is that you should find your best skills that make you stand out as a leader, and then impart them to others within the organisation and making sure that they are equipped to effectively use them. Doing this involves risk because all your employees will not achieve the same result, but you can be sure that in the end, your investment will be more than you doing it alone.

The main point here is that as a leader, you will at some stage need to ask yourself if your kind of leadership has the ability to transform the organisation and make it the front runner in its area of specialisation. If the answer is yes, then in order to achieve this, you will need to consciously seek to convert every organisational "servant" into a leader ("trader"). How can this be done? Train them to develop and manage a core talent essential to the success of your business.

Nevertheless *(verses 26-30)*, you also need to deal with your non-performing assets *(that is, the man who hid his talent)*. Talent, is never given for wasting, and in the same manner that God will require you to account for yours someday, you must also ensure that there is accountability from those to whom you gave your talents.

After all, this is the business of God and God does not waste anything, neither should you.

Principle 52

THE DYNAMICS OF LEADERSHIP POWER

Mathew 26: 45 – 54

Then He came to His disciples and said to them, "Are you still sleeping and resting? Behold, the hour is at hand, and the Son of Man is being betrayed into the hands of sinners. [46] Rise, let us be going. See, My betrayer is at hand." [47] And while He was still speaking, behold, Judas, one of the twelve, with a great multitude with swords and clubs, came from the chief priests and elders of the people. [48] Now His betrayer had given them a sign, saying, "Whomever I kiss, He is the One; seize Him." [49] Immediately he went up to Jesus and said, "Greetings, Rabbi!" and kissed Him. [50] But Jesus said to him, "Friend, why have you come?" Then they came and laid hands on Jesus and took Him. [51] And suddenly, one of those who were with Jesus stretched out his hand and drew his sword, struck the servant of the high priest, and cut off his ear. [52] But Jesus said to him, "Put your sword in its place, for all who take the sword will perish by the sword. [53] Or do you think that I cannot now pray to My Father, and He will provide Me with more than twelve legions of angels? 54 How then could the Scriptures be fulfilled, that it must happen thus?"

Not everyone knows how to exercise power correctly and for those of who have power, you should find the lessons revealed from the above text useful.

Many people with some "power" believe that consistently exercising it at every given opportunity is the way to consolidate it. Sometimes, real power requires that you subdue the urge to exercise it even when an opportunity presents itself. This is usually done in order gain an even greater power. The power here, in the business sense could mean having an edge in business.

In the passage above, we read the story of Jesus' arrest leading up to His crucifixion.

The paradox to this arrest is that several times in the Bible, one reads about how Jesus escaped the throng of people or elders of the Jews plotting to kill Him. So we are forced to ask why did Jesus, who knew Judas had betrayed Him, go to an isolated place where Judas knew He could be found. Furthermore, we are left to wonder why Jesus, the son of God, did not at the time of his arrest call for re-enforcements from heaven or earth even though He had the power to do so.

Instead, he refused to exercise His power, allowing Himself to be taken away in a manner that was sure to make satan feel more powerful than He. However, by choosing not to exercise His power, getting crucified, buried and resurrected, He obtained the greatest power of all. By doing this, satan is now placed underneath His feet and every knee will have to bow to Jesus as Lord.

Here are two key lessons:

(i) Firstly, allowing someone else to appear more powerful than you are, when in real terms you have what it takes to exercise equal or greater power over them, puts that person in a position of vulnerability since they tend to feel superior, leading to complacency and a dropping of their guards. This act of carelessness can provide the opportunity to gain mastery and advantage over them.

(ii) Secondly, where exercising your power in a present moment will hinder the attainment of a greater prize, Christ-like wisdom demands you consider restraining the use of such power in order to obtain the greater prize.

Principle 53

MITIGATING ORGANISATIONAL LOSSES

Mark 5: 25 – 35

[25] Now a certain woman had a flow of blood for twelve years, [26] and had suffered many things from many physicians. She had spent all that she had and was no better, but rather grew worse. [27] When she heard about Jesus, she came behind Him in the crowd and touched His garment. [28] For she said, "If only I may touch His clothes, I shall be made well." [29] Immediately the fountain of her blood was dried up, and she felt in her body that she was healed of the affliction. [30] And Jesus, immediately knowing in Himself that power had gone out of Him, turned around in the crowd and said, "Who touched My clothes?" [31] But His disciples said to Him, "You see the multitude thronging You, and You say, 'Who touched Me?'"[32] And He looked around to see her who had done this thing. [33] But the woman, fearing and trembling, knowing what had happened to her, came and fell down before Him and told Him the whole truth. [34] And He said to her, "Daughter, your faith has made you well. Go in peace, and be healed of your affliction." [35] While He was

still speaking, some came from the ruler of the synagogue's house who said, "Your daughter is dead. Why trouble the Teacher any further?"

Bible says, *"the life of every man is in the blood."* Every institution and political system has some form of "blood" running through it. If that life force is drained out, that institution or system is dead.

In the above passage, Jesus' encounter with the woman who had an issue of blood teaches us about a fundamental principle that is required by all entities in order to maintain a hold on their lead, their excellence, superiority or whatever it is that sets them apart from others.

Here, Jesus shows that every effort you put into ensuring you remain in the lead must be equally matched with efforts to ensure nothing beneficial to you leaves through the backdoor unchecked.

Let me explain. Imagine a Ferrari sports car on a highway at the speed of 300 kilometres per hour and a leak in the fuel pipe is letting out fuel at the rate of 10 gallons per kilometre. Imagine further that there is nothing on your dashboard warning you of your fuel leak. You and I will both agree the Ferrari won't travel beyond the 7 kilometre mark before it grinds to a halt.

Before this incident, Jesus had preached in several places where multitudes thronged Him. After this incident He still preached in many places where He had to wade through multitudes, but it was only on this one occasion that He turned around from His ministration to ask the big question - "*who touched Me?*"

Why? Because on all the other occasions before and after this incident, His ministration involved giving out what HE wanted to give out. Each time He healed someone, or cast out a demon, He knew what He was giving out of His store of virtue. Only on this occasion was virtue drawn out of Him without His consent – that's why he noticed it so quickly.

Most importantly, what it shows business owners and leaders is that Jesus had a system for effectively identifying "*unapproved*" leakages. For Him to leave the act of healing in the middle, to find out why something He had not willingly approved had left Him, is proof that He attached equal importance to His ministry of "giving" as He did the systems in place to stop unwarranted losses. In the same vein, successful business leaders should have such systems in place:

1. Firstly, take the time to understand your business or the institution that you are leading and identify what your lifelines are. For Jesus, it was the divine virtue flowing through Him. Therefore, we need to ask what the core

components of an organisation's successes are. What is that key organisational component which if removed will certainly cause its collapse.

For a business, it may be your cash flow, your qualified core personnel, or your product patent. For the institution you are leading, it may be your operational strategy or your contacts in the industry.

2. Secondly, explore the various ways these core elements can be cut off from your business or institution without your knowledge or consent.

3. Once you have considered the above two, develop clear and effective systems to detect and prevent such losses. Notice that the disciples were Jesus' preventive mechanism. Because they failed to prevent the woman from drawing virtue from Him, His own detection systems picked it up. Also notice that as soon as Jesus detected virtue had left Him, the first thing He did was to go back to the preventive system *(His disciples)* to figure out why this first line of defence was breached.

4. Design ahead of time the specific actions to be taken when there is a breach of preventive or detection systems.

Principle 54

CONTINUOUS CHANGE MANAGEMENT

Mathew 9: 16 – 17

[16] *No one puts a piece of unshrunk cloth on an old garment; for the patch pulls away from the garment, and the tear is made worse.* [17] *Nor do they put new wine into old wine-skins, or else the wineskins break, the wine is spilled, and the wineskins are ruined. But they put new wine into new wineskins, and both are preserved."*

1 Chronicles 12: 32

[32] *Of the sons of Issachar who had understanding of the times, to know what Israel ought to do, their chiefs were two hundred; and all their brethren were at their command.*

Whether you are in business or in leadership there are a few things that need to be established before I share one of the most exciting business and leadership wisdoms. They are:

- Every business enterprises always has competition in one form or another and the only sure way to beat your competition at all times is to always stay ahead of them. This way, it is they who will have to do a lot of work to try and catch up with you.

- Change will always happen and, usually, those who embrace change achieve success. In the past, however, we have seen where change, if effected wrongly, can easily destroy an otherwise successful organisation or reduce its effectiveness so that it loses its competitive edge to others who have been better able to implement change correctly. The resultant loss of leadership could arise from the fact that in the past, change was viewed and responded to wrongly.

- Under these circumstances, leadership is seen in a more restrictive sense to mean being ahead of the game with everyone else following in your wake. The hard truth is that if you are not leading, then you are following, and those who follow do not make the rules for everyone else.

By the Grace of God Almighty, I am about to show you a ridiculously simple system that will ensure that in whatever area of business, leadership or politics that you find yourself:

(i) you can consistently win out over your competition (ii) you are managing change very effectively and efficiently and, alongside all these (iii) you also remain in a leading position. Yes, indeed, all these three things are achievable on a day to day basis.

The different pieces of cloth and wines referred to in the passage from Matthew relate to the different dispensations of time. The passage emphasises that timings are different and so are the things that need to be done in each of the individual timing. In other words, what used to be done in the past cannot be done exactly the same way in the present with the expectation of achieving the same results. In fact, sometimes even the results in each dispensation should not be expected to be the same. For example, in the area of politics or even advertising, in the past customers and voters were reached with information coming primarily from TV, radio, flyers and personal appearances. In today's society, mobile phones and the social media are two of the primary means being used. In order to be on the cutting edge as a business leader who is consistently ahead of your opponents, you must effectively embrace and manage change. You will need to develop a culture of consistently asking the following two questions on a regular basis:

1. What period of time are we now in and is what we are doing now appropriate for this time?

2. What future period of time are current trends pointing to and what are we presently doing that needs to be changed in order for us to have the ultimate advantage when this expected period becomes a reality? (1 Chronicles 12: 32).

We cannot continue to deal with change as we did in the past when we continued doing things in the same old way until the need for change was inevitable. Then we would, at a given point in time, shutdown all our old ways of doing things and carry out one big overhaul to bring us in line with the new approaches. This approach makes change cumbersome, complicated and sometimes ineffective. By asking the above questions regularly at all strategic levels, two things are bound to happen:

1. You will always be thinking about and effecting change in small manageable bits.

2. You will always be ready to reap the advantages of a new age before many others and this is what will make you lead and others follow.

Principle 55

HANDLING PUBLIC RELATIONS OR PUBLICITY

Mark 5: 11 – 20

Now a large herd of swine was feeding there near the mountains. [12] So all the demons begged Him, saying, "Send us to the swine, that we may enter them." [13] And at once Jesus[a] gave them permission. Then the unclean spirits went out and entered the swine (there were about two thousand); and the herd ran violently down the steep place into the sea, and drowned in the sea. [14] So those who fed the swine fled, and they told it in the city and in the country. And they went out to see what it was that had happened. [15] Then they came to Jesus, and saw the one who had been demon-possessed and had the legion, sitting and clothed and in his right mind. And they were afraid. [16] And those who saw it told them how it happened to him who had been demon-possessed, and about the swine. [17] Then they began to plead with Him to depart from their region. [18] And when He got into the boat, he who had been demon-possessed begged Him that he might be with Him. [19] However, Jesus did not permit him, but said to him, "Go home to your friends, and tell them what great things the Lord has done for you, and how He has had compassion on you." [20] *And he departed and began to proclaim in Decapolis all that Jesus had done for him; and all marvelled*

For any successful business, institutional or political leader, there comes a time when one will need to engage in one form of the other of public relations.

You might decide to do it yourself or hand it over to your staff or a specialist firm, but whichever the case, some basic rules still apply. Public relations are about managing information between you, your organisation and the public.

Although the lessons from the passage above relate primarily to public relations, I am convinced that the principle can be applied in many other areas where these three parameters are present: (i) your organisation (ii) the public - anybody or thing outside the organisation, and (iii) information dissemination.

In the above passage, Jesus shows us that if you can control the four key elements of any public relation activity, it will be successful. These key elements are:

1. ***You must control the destination targeted by the information dissemination:*** The fully healed man requested to travel with Jesus to wherever He was going, but Jesus specifically required of him to go to the Decapolis and spread the news there. Understand that not every public relation activity is applicable to all destination or demographics. Yes, it may be the same information, crafted in the same language, to be disseminated through the same outlet, but it may not necessarily be the right one for all target destinations or demographics.

2. ***You must control who does the dissemination:*** There were onlookers at the time Jesus cast out the demons from the possessed man but He never commissioned any of them to carry the news anywhere. He wisely commissioned someone who had a more intimate connection with the information *He* wanted publicized. This is why sometimes I have a bit of a problem with organisations, which when designing a marketing campaign for a new product, totally omit the inputs of their technical teams who intimately know the product – because they made it. The wisdom is that because of the knowledge and experience they possess, some people, more than others, will make a greater impact in communicating certain types of information.

3. ***You must control information content disseminated:*** We see in the text above, Jesus clearly defines for the healed man, the exact framework within which he must disseminate his testimony. He is instructed to declare only what great things the Lord has done for him and the compassion He has had on him. Nothing more, nothing less.

4. ***You must control beforehand, who is to be targeted to receive the information:*** In the passage above, Jesus specifically told the man to go to his friends and disseminate the news to them. This should lead you to ask: if this this man had been demon possessed for a long time, who were the friends to whom he was being sent? Are these people who were also demon possessed?

Principle 56

PROFITING BEYOND BOOK-PROFITS

Luke 5: 3 – 10

3 *Then He got into one of the boats, which was Simon's, and*
asked him to put out a little from the land. And He sat
down and taught the multitudes from the boat. 4 *When He*
had stopped speaking, He said to Simon, "Launch out into
the deep and let down your nets for a catch." 5 *But Simon*
answered and said to Him, "Master, we have toiled all night
and caught nothing; nevertheless at Your word I will let
down the net." 6 *And when they had done this, they caught*
a great number of fish, and their net was breaking. 7 *So they*
signalled to their partners in the other boat to come and
help them. And they came and filled both the boats, so that
they began to sink. 8 *When Simon Peter saw it, he fell down*
at Jesus' knees, saying, "Depart from me, for I am a sinful
man, O Lord!" 9 *For he and all who were with him were*
astonished at the catch of fish which they had taken; 10 *and*
so also were James and John, the sons of Zebedee, who were
partners with Simon. And Jesus said to Simon, "Do not be
afraid. From now on you will catch men."

From a practical perspective, it is possible as a Christian to unconsciously continue your personal walk of faith with God and yet, divorce Him from your business operations and your institutional or political leadership duties.

The secular world has succeeded in teaching us their way of doing business, with no God in it, so much so that, we only tend to look at profitability to believe a secular school of thought. Sadly in the process, we cast aside our own Godly systems of doing business, which not only generate better gains, but are also backed by the blessings of God, to defy many failures.

When one uses the business systems of man, one only gets man-made guarantees which do not necessarily deliver what they promise. On the other hand, when you use the systems of God, you get a God-guarantee covering the system's performance, its profitability and durability. It really is a matter of choice.

Let's consider some analogies here: every business and leadership role we are engaged in has the core agenda of serving the needs of mankind. As a result, profitability in business is somewhat generated from the price mankind is willing to pay for their needs being satisfied.

God is a righteous, faithful and a very business oriented

God. If a business is involved any way in satisfying His needs, there is no way He will cheat and not pay for His needs being satisfied.

Think about it. In the passage above we learn these two lessons:

1. Simon, upon the instructions of Jesus, let down his net into the deep and made the biggest catch and profit as a fisherman. If I was to ask how Simon made that catch, I am most likely to be answered – *"he was obedient"* or *"because Jesus was in the boat"*. Those may be true too. Up to this point however, Simon had always been following Jesus and he had always been obedient *(the bible doesn't say the contrary)*. Also, Jesus could have equally worked this miracle without necessarily sitting in Simon's boat *(just like he ordered Peter to go to the lake in Matthew chapter 17, to take money out of a fish's mouth for the settlement of their temple taxes)*.

   Revelation tells me, that the real reason Simon made such a huge catch was because his business *(boat)* satisfied a need of God *(to be used for preaching)* and as a result, he had to be paid – not in currency but with blessings. Yes of course, the payment for the use of his boat was more than usual because:

(i) whether you serve man or God, you will get paid but
(ii) man or God can only make a payment to the extent of their respective possessions
(iii) man only possesses what God has put in his hands; God on the other hand possesses all things.

This last point accounts for why the reward from God exceeds that which Simon had been receiving from mankind *(human efforts)* all this while.

2. Another lesson to learn from this passage is that God has multiple graces and as a result, there is more than one way He can sovereignly choose to pay you for using your business or leadership abilities to satisfy His needs. He can choose to pay you in the form of physical riches, in mental and physical security or in an anointing, but you can be sure of one thing – His payment will be in line with your type of business or purpose. For Simon, a fisherman, it was fish.

   More often than not, these blessings *(rewards)* are expressed by God in the form of specific guidance where He speaks to you directly *(through revelations, dreams, other encounters)* or through His servants. Many Christians, however, find it difficult to recognize when God has spoken.

When God speaks, you will be sure to find three elements in His communication, just as they appeared in the passage when Jesus spoke to Simon:

- He will tell you exactly where to go - *(He asked Simon to Launch into the deep)*
- He will tell you what you are to do once you get there - *(He asks Simon to let down his nets)*, and finally
- He will tell you the outcome of your obedience - *(He tells Simon he will have a catch)*

Remember, whether in business, or in leadership – your profitability or rewards arise from satisfying someone else's needs. For mere profitability, you can choose to satisfy the needs of mankind. For extraordinary profitability and rewards, you should consider also satisfying the needs of Jesus, the Christ.

I'll leave this section by answering that nagging question on someone's mind: "what is the need of Jesus Christ?" The need of our Lord here on earth is for His gospel of salvation and the word of God to reach all the ends of the earth.

Principle 57

DIFFERENT METHODS OF PROBLEM SOLVING

Luke 18: 35 – 43

*[35] Then it happened, as He was coming near Jericho, that a
certain blind man sat by the road begging. [36] And hearing
a multitude passing by, he asked what it meant. [37] So they
told him that Jesus of Nazareth was passing by. [38] And he
cried out, saying, "Jesus, Son of David, have mercy on me!"
[39] Then those who went before warned him that he should
be quiet; but he cried out all the more, "Son of David, have
mercy on me!" [40] So Jesus stood still and commanded him to
be brought to Him. And when he had come near, He asked
him, [41] saying, "What do you want Me to do for you?" He
said, "Lord, that I may receive my sight." [42] Then Jesus said
to him, "Receive your sight; your faith has made you well."
[43] And immediately he received his sight, and followed Him,
glorifying God. And all the people, when they saw it, gave
praise to God.*

Problem-solving is an everyday occurrence for any business owner. Indeed, it is also one of the foundation upon which leadership is built.

Over the years, however, the vast majority of leaders and business people have come to accept that being in the position of a problem-solver requires that one has to go looking for solutions. This is not entirely true.

The above text, a very popular story in the Bible, teaches us more than one way to carry out problem-solving. The eye, in scripture, mostly represents one's ability to see, to seek, to visualize and to focus. It is thus easy to understand why the act of being a problem-solver concentrates much on one's ability to "*visualise*" the problem in order to understand it and, once understood, to focus on seeking a solution for it. It ticks all the right boxes for the primary utilisation of your physical, spiritual and mental eye.

Sadly, however, and human as we are, one's physical, spiritual and mental vision can and will be impaired from time to time by things like stress and health problems, spiritual fall, etc. These human weaknesses however do not prevent problems from arising. Instead, they only impair one's ability visualize and understand problems, thus impairing our ability to solve them.

Conversely, when a leader or business owner's focus, visualisation and vision are at their best, there is really little problem with finding a solution. Although our visions will not always be at their best, it shouldn't mean our ability to find solutions be hindered.

Let's go back to the story of the blind man. From the onset we understand he had no sight, so he could not locate where solution was *(i.e. where Jesus was standing in the crowd)*, let alone, go forth to take it *(i.e. receive his solution of healing)*. But he did something extraordinary – he called out to the solution. As a result, he did not have to see, locate and walk to the solution; the solution requested an audience with him. In other words, the solution came to him. A few practical lessons to learn, irrespective of our visual impairments:

1. You must train yourself to listen for solutions in the most unlikely places. As with the blind man, he must have figured just by listening very carefully, that the crowd seemed to carry a different energy on this particular day – otherwise, how would he have known that Jesus, son of David was the one causing a stir in the energy of the crowd *(Jesus never announced Himself – so how else did he know?)*

2. Calling in solutions is the critical alternative to seeking solutions visually, and it involves using our mouth. One of the primary ways of using your mouth in this context is TO PRAY. Yes, Pray. Samson did the same when his vision was taken from him. He used his mouth in prayer and the Lord gave him back his strength.

   But it is not all about prayer. In our modern world, we find we can also use our "virtual" mouths to call out to our solution by effectively using the media in all its various forms. Use of the media is not confined to journalists or solely to having your message transmitted only by radio and TV. Instead, it embraces the use of everything audio, visual and graphic as well as the internet, all of which can be deployed to amplify what you really want to say to the world, including asking for a solution, that most likely may be roaming somewhere out there in the world..

3. When the potential source of your required solution does meet with you, you must be ready with a clear concise expression of your need – just as in the case of the blind man. When he was asked what solution he needed, he didn't mince his words – he was precise, concise and to the point.

Principle 58

HOW TO FISH FOR OPTIMUM OPPORTUNITIES

Numbers 32: 1 – 6, 16 – 19

Now the children of Reuben and the children of Gad had a very great multitude of livestock; and when they saw the land of Jazer and the land of Gilead, that indeed the region was a place for livestock, [2] the children of Gad and the children of Reuben came and spoke to Moses, to Eleazar the priest, and to the leaders of the congregation, saying, [3] "Ataroth, Dibon, Jazer, Nimrah, Heshbon, Elealeh, Shebam, Nebo, and Beon, [4] the country which the Lord defeated before the congregation of Israel, is a land for livestock, and your servants have livestock." [5] Therefore they said, "If we have found favour in your sight, let this land be given to your servants as a possession. Do not take us over the Jordan." [6] And Moses said to the children of Gad and to the children of Reuben: "Shall your brethren go to war while you sit here?

16 Then they came near to him and said: "We will build sheepfolds here for our livestock, and cities for our little ones,
17 but we ourselves will be armed, ready to go before the children of Israel until we have brought them to their place; and our little ones will dwell in the fortified cities because of the inhabitants of the land.
18 We will not return to our homes until every one of the children of Israel has received his inheritance.
19 For we will not inherit with them on the other side of the Jordan and beyond, because our inheritance has fallen to us on this eastern side of the Jordan."

As a leader or business person, you will be faced with opportunities every now and again. Knowing the right opportunities to take and at what time to take them will determine your organisation's success or failure.

More often than not, the choice a leader makes, in terms of which opportunities he takes or rejects, is often influenced to a large extent by what everybody else is doing, where the trend is leading and where the most respected pacesetters of the industry are headed. However, making choices based solely on these factors can lead to disaster because this is certainly NOT the best way to decide which opportunity to take. From the passage above, we can learn how.

Taking an opportunity does not necessarily mean going where everybody is headed. Note that all the children of Israel were intended to cross over the Jordan and the tribes of Reuben and Gad should have done so too – but they decided otherwise. These two tribes came to the rare understanding that everybody else's opportunity does not equate to their opportunity. Opportunity is not always the place everybody else believes there is milk and honey or where the majority believe they can flourish.

Opportunity is the place where: (i) your strengths can be sustained to flourish longer (ii) where your strength receives more value.

Reuben and Gad identified that their strengths lay in their possession of great multitudes of livestock. Because they understood this, they could recognize that Canaan, the land flowing with milk and honey, was NOT "their" opportunity but, that their real opportunity was in the land of Jazer – for the exact two reasons I shared above: (i) Firstly, their livestock could not be sustained nor flourish by feeding on honey and milk in Canaan as compared to the readily available pastures in Jazer which was very suitable for cattle (ii) Canaan was already flowing with milk which would mean that their multitude of livestock would be less valuable in Canaan. The basic rules of demand and supply are in play here – Canaan already had a lot of cattle *(i.e.*

flowing with milk), so if Gad and Reuben drove their cattle there, there would have been a greater supply of cattle or milk than demand and hence, their livestock values would have plummeted.

Another business and leadership lesson we can learn from this passage is this – to preserve your own opportunities, help those who would have shared your opportunities with you to find theirs elsewhere, away from yours. That's exactly what Reuben and Gad did - they helped the other children of Israel to cross over the Jordan into Canaan, away from Jazer.

Principle 59

OPTIMIZING WEALTH AND INVESTMENT PORTFOLIO

Job 1: 1 – 3

There was a man in the land of Uz, whose name was Job; and that man was blameless and upright, and one who feared God and shunned evil. [2] And seven sons and three daughters were born to him. [3] Also, his possessions were seven thousand sheep, three thousand camels, five hundred yoke of oxen, five hundred female donkeys, and a very large household, so that this man was the greatest of all the people of the East.

Job 42: 12 – 15

[12] Now the Lord blessed the latter days of Job more than his beginning; for he had fourteen thousand sheep, six thousand camels, one thousand yoke of oxen, and one thousand female donkeys. [13] He also had seven sons and three daughters. [14] And he called the name of the first Jemimah, the name of the second Keziah, and the name of the third Keren-Happuch. [15] In all the land were found no women so beautiful as the daughters of Job; and their father gave them an inheritance among their brothers.

Reading the two passages in Job chapters 1 and 42, the two big things that become apparent is the fact that in both texts, the number of sons and daughters of Job remain the same – seven sons and three daughters. The only other very obvious occurrence is that the numbers of different animals in chapter 42 is exactly twice the number of animals in chapter 1.

But beyond all of these, there is something amazingly technical God is trying to show every business person, leader and individual for that matter – it's about how to invest in the right proportions. For those mathematically inclined, you will have already worked out the following ratios in the animals

- 14,000 Sheep = 63%
- 6,000 Camel = 27%
- 1,000 Oxen = 5%
- 1,000 Female Donkeys = 5%

In chapter 1, this is the structure of the wealth possessed by the wise Job. The question anyone should be asking is – why did God, when increasing Job's wealth in chapter 42, retains the same proportions? The answer is – this system of wealth apportionment was taught to Job by God Himself through

Abel, the son of Adam. It is Godly and it is universal in both the physical and spiritual realm. Now let's delve into the understanding behind the ratios:

1. ***63% of your wealth must always be in trading.*** That is to say it must be involved in everyday business ventures and activities. Everyday means between the hours when the day begins and when it closes at night *(just like a shop opens and closes)*, 63% of your wealth should be engaged in multiple trading. Of all the animals Job had, the sheep were the only ones that could be traded on a daily and regular basis for the continued increase of his income. Because of its size and daily usefulness, the sheep itself could be sold, as well as its wool for making clothing and its hide for leather – that is multiple trading. There are multiple incomes from sheep, meaning that it represents industry and enterprise.

   Besides this, of all the animals listed, sheep have the shortest gestation period of approximately 150 days making its rate of reproduction or generation of business profit higher. Interestingly, the Hebrew equivalent of the word sheep is "*TSON*" and the individual letters that make up the word mean the following: *a place, selling, open and close and new* – I will leave your imaginations to figure out the rest.

2. ***Camels are always representative of property***, and this is used to advise us that 27% of our wealth should be invested in property *(especially land)* or any such investment that performs like real estate, *e.g. gold*. Here are a few very basic similarities you may find interesting.

   Camels by their nature are always rising from the ground – consider how the value of land, for the most part, is always rising and hardly ever falling. I am an accountant and I can tell you that on any organisation's balance sheet, minimum justification is needed to explain why the value of land has increased, but, on the contrary, a disproportionately higher justification is needed to prove that the value of land has fallen. Also consider that a camel is the only animal that performs best in the desert, and in sandstorms – likewise land, as a property, is the one investment in the whole universe that retains its value performance even in the midst of financial droughts or economic sandstorms.

3. ***Hold 5% of your investments in cash***. The Hebrew word for oxen comes from the root word "*BAQAR*" which means to *seek, inquire or consider*. This means that you need to hold this percentage of your wealth in very liquid form to take advantage *(i.e. to seek and consider)* of quick, profitable business or investment opportunities that come

around from time to time and will only be accessible to those who have immediate access to funds. The interesting thing about these opportunities is that they are not available for long and may disappear by the time you are able to convert your non-liquid assets in order to take advantage of them.

4. ***Finally, keep your remaining 5% of wealth in very long term investments***. Why do I say that? The animal, donkey or ass, generally represent long enduring patience indeed. So we are talking about investments that you can hang on to over the very long term.

   A donkey may be slow, but it will go the longest distance, take every burden you place on it, receive all the beating and yet, never fight back. That is the nature of a long term investment.

   The word for ass/donkey in Hebrew is "*EYTHAN*" and is translated into English as meaning *"perpetual, constant and ever-flowing"*. If you note carefully, this is the only animal in the list that is specified as females. This means that they must be the type of long term investments *(e.g. shares and stocks and bonds)* that are perpetually producing constant incomes or gains.

Finally, the passage tells us that 70% of his children are men and 30% are women. And if you noted rightly, this proportion never changed irrespective of the number of the animals Job possessed before and after his fall. Men establish, maintain, perpetuate; women grow and expand. Adam was commanded to *"keep" (till)* the garden *(establish, maintain, keep intact)*; Eve on the other hand after they left Eden, birthed Cain and Abel and later, Seth therefore expanding the lineage and heritage of Adam *(growth, expansion, increase, multiplication).*

And here's the secret: the Hebrew words for son and daughter are respectively *"BEN"* and *"BATH"* and both come from the root word *"BANA"*. The masculine arm *(i.e. Ben)* of this word "Bana" means "establish" and the feminine arm of it *(i.e. Bath)* means "to continue building". The meaning is that in order to perpetuate your riches to become sustainable wealth, 70% and 30% of your efforts respectively should be focused on establishing and growing.

Effectively 70% of your riches invested in quick turn-around investments *(i.e. sheep and Oxen)* is what ensures the maintenance of your wealth's value; and 30% of your longer reach investments *(i.e. Camel and female donkeys)*, is what guarantees perpetual growth in the value of your wealth.

You should also apply this principle even if you intend to recruit a fund management team to manage your wealth.

Principle 60

THE FORMULA FOR CREATING EVERYTHING

Genesis 1: 3 – 24

[3] Then God said, "Let there be light"; and there was light.....

[6] Then God said, "Let there be a firmament in the midst of the waters, and let it divide the waters from the waters."

[9] Then God said, "Let the waters under the heavens be gathered together into one place, and let the dry land appear"; and it was so.

[14] Then God said, "Let there be lights in the firmament of the heavens to divide the day from the night; and let them be for signs and seasons, and for days and years; [15] and let them be for lights in the firmament of the heavens to give light on the earth";

[20] Then God said, "Let the waters abound with an abundance of living creatures......

[24] Then God said, "Let the earth bring forth the living creature according to its kind: cattle and creeping thing and beast of the earth, each according to its kind"; and it was so.

In general, God went through six stages in building the earth from formless chaos. This is the master-plan in building everything else here on earth, including businesses and institutions. The main stages of the process involved:

Day 1 – Light
Day 2 – Creation of the Firmament
Day 3 – Gathering the seas to reveal the earth
Day 4 – Lights in the firmament
Day 5 – Sea creatures are created
Day 6 – Earth creatures are created

In every building process here on earth and with special reference to businesses, organisations and political entities, these six distinct stages must be applied. In its absence, you can be sure that whatever you are building will have defects that will cost you in the future. Now, the six stages:

Stage 1: Light

Irrespective of what you are building, the first stage is always one for enlightenment, meaning you are required to enlighten yourself about what you are intending to build by gleaning as much knowledge as you can about it. Firstly the vision (the greatest light) for what you are about to build from God – what is the godly insight about it? What purpose has been revealed to you about what you intend to build?

Then of course the earthly light – what do you know about what you want to build? Everything? Nobody is asking you to be a professional in every department but you NEED to have some knowledge about them and this must be acquired by reading, researching, asking questions of those who are experts and, if need be, attending courses and seminars to educate yourself. Altogether, these will provide the light you need to undertake the venture.

If God saw the need to turn on the lights before starting His creation work, there is every excellent reason that you should turn yours on too.

Stage 2 – Creation of the Firmament:

The creation of the firmament depicts the establishment of firm structures and dependable systems that define the way things should consistently be done as well as when and why.

The firmament also defines the language of the business, organisation or power entity.

The purpose of the firmament is to ensure all the people within a business, organisation or power hierarchy collectively speak the same language and do things the same or structured but creative way, thereby establishing the structures that set such an entity apart from all the others. If you think about it, most organisations in the same industry are likely to be engaged in the same operations – but the actual manner in which those operations are carried out is what sets each organisation apart from the other.

Firmaments are like the walls and doors in an office building – they are firm enough to ensure that: (i) you stay within your allocated area most of the times and (ii) that you do not stray at will from the general staff area into the Director's office. Note that in the Bible text, *the firmament divides the waters above from the waters beneath.*

This signifies that the firmament is a firm enough structure for the leadership at the top *(waters above)* to rest on, knowing that their policies and directives, once set in motion will provide some degree of predictability of operations and result they can rely on to move the entity forward.

It is also a dependable system for the workers or followers in the lower ranks *(the waters below)* to draw inspiration from – just like the rivers and lakes on earth below, depend on the rains from the clouds above *(the water system above)* to get filled or topped up from time to time.

It is essential, therefore, in designing structures and systems *(i.e. the firmament)* that one bears in mind that it should not only work well for those at the top, it should also work for those below.

Stage 3 – Gathering the seas to reveal the earth:

This stage refers to strategically organising your departments into which your work forces will eventually settle into when recruited. Understand that prior to this stage, the land and the waters were all together and that it was only after all the waters were gathered together as sea, and the land together as earth, that God was able to cause each of them to start bearing fruits and life forms as we would see in stages 5 and 6.

The basic principle is that when building your work force: (i) systems should already have been put in place and (ii) teams should be created on the principle of all *"all like together"*. This is the basis for the creation of departments where people carrying out similar activities are grouped together.

The important lesson from this is that when recruiting people, consider selecting and assigning them based on their specialisations, as this will lead to greater productivity. The onus is on you to ensure that each staff member is placed where he or she will perform optimally, and this decision is yours to make, not the employee's.

To look at this another way, the sea is fluid and expansive hence why it is the perfect environment for equally streamlined and free-flowing creatures like fish that are always eager to swim into every available sea space. The land is rigid and resolute, hence why it is equally suited to creatures that are very structured in their natures. Trying to have the sea or its suited creatures take the place of the land and its creatures will end up making both redundant and wasted.

The clear distinction between land and sea also explains a critical concept in creating departments: (i) some departments will act as land – these are the departments that provide the stability for the organisation or business. Elsewhere, these are referred to as the support departments. They are quite immovable and are not the departments that determine when or how a business or organisation changes direction. On the other hand, (ii) some departments will act like the sea – fluid, always in motion, changing according to the tide.

The latter, are the departments that determine the direction in which the whole organisation goes. So, if your organisation is a product- oriented one, then, your design department for example is likely to be the most fluid unit, and likewise if your organisation is a political party with a philosophical emphasis on the economy rather than military prowess, then it is likely that your economic research and strategy team will be the driving force.

Just like the sea which is always looking for dry ground to fill up, these are departments that are always on the prowl for new opportunities and depending on what those opportunities turn out to be, the entire organisation will have to follow.

Stage 4 – Lights in the upper firmament:

This stage of the building process also involves knowledge of some sort, but not of the kind referred to in stage 1 above. At this level, the knowledge being referred to is "*the casting of a vision*". Note that the Bible refers to light being established in the upper levels above the firmament and for these lights to now provide light to the earth below. This means that the earth below does not have any light of its own but the light it needs is provided it from the enlightened matter in the upper firmament.

Here is the understanding - the leaders at the top are enlightened with the *vision* of the business, organisation or power movement. This is not a mere process of telling senior management what the overall vision is, instead, it is about consciously making them the "*owners*" of the vision *(just as Bible says the moon and sun were established in the higher firmament region)*. By this enlightenment, they will in turn provide visionary leadership to their respective departments or units below *(just as the sun and moon shine their light on the earth).*

The presence of the two types of lights, that is, the sun and the moon, does not necessarily mean a leadership team of your organisation needs to be made to own two different types of vision – it simply means that whatever vision they own has to dynamic enough to provide a guiding light in different seasons. Just like the sun and the moon both provide light, but of different types and at different times of the day.

There will be day times and night periods and the vision should be versatile enough to provide clear direction in all these different seasons.

Stage 5 – Sea creatures are created:

This stage refers directly to the people in the departments that lead the entire organisation.

The important recognition here is that this department *(the sea)* is being populated before the stable, more rigid departments *(land)* for that very reason – the former, is the department that leads for the whole organisation to follow and as such, must be populated first to lead the remainder of the entity building process.

You may have already noticed that most of the creatures that populate the sea tend to have a similarly streamlined and fluid body design to enable them live comfortably in the water. This is to stress that people who are fluid in their nature, thinking and creativity should be recruited into the actual departments that determine the movement or progress of the entire organisation.

Stage 6 – Land creatures are created:

This stage is the exact opposite reflection of everything presented in stage 5 above.

As a framework, these are the six core building stages that any business, organisation, and power movements needs to engage in as core building blocks. Of course, depending on the nature of the entity, other things will be added but the structure above should, if possible, retained as the master plan and the rest, elevation plans.

AUTHOR'S OTHER WORKS

Title:	Is This Why Africa Is? (E-book & Paperback)
Description:	I ask all the questions about Africa that nobody else will. Deep, profound questions
Availability:	Amazon & Kindle
Link to View:	http://goo.gl/ecRMig

Title:	Where Did God Hide His Diamonds? (E-book & Paperback)
Description:	Discovering what exactly God has hidden in you, finding it & prospering freely from it
Availability:	Amazon & Kindle
Link to View:	http://goo.gl/ecRMig

Title:	Doing Business with God (E-book & Paperback)
Description:	60 shocking biblical principles for extraordinary leadership, business and politics.
Availability:	Amazon & Kindle
Link to View:	http://goo.gl/ecRMig

Title:	Midnight Philosophies (E-book & Paperback)
Description:	My Deep thoughts, Philosophies, Reflections – Whispers of my mind.
Availability:	Amazon & Kindle
Link to View:	http://goo.gl/ecRMig

Title:	This Godly Child of Mine (E-book & Paperback)
Description:	A revelatory book on how to raise godly children in a perverse and lawless world
Availability:	Amazon & Kindle
Link to View:	http://goo.gl/ecRMig

Title:	The Deputy Minister for Corruption (E-book & Paperback)
Description:	A Novel
Availability:	Amazon & Kindle
Link to View:	http://goo.gl/ecRMig

Title:	A Dove in the Storm (E-book & Paperback)
Description:	A Novel
Availability:	Amazon & Kindle
Link to View:	http://goo.gl/ecRMig

Title:	100% JOB INTERVIEW SUCCESS (E-book & Paperback)
Description:	A simple, straightforward guide to passing every job interview you attend.
Availability:	Amazon & Kindle
Link to View:	http://goo.gl/ecRMig

Title:	Bible-by-Heart (Mobile App)
Description:	A simple but effective App to help anyone memorize 500 Bible verses in a year.
Availability:	iTunes & Google Play Stores

Link to View:	http://goo.gl/T3UdPN (i-Tunes)
Link to View:	http://goo.gl/ljnECR (Android)

Title:	Holy Rat (Mobile Game)
Description:	An exciting Christian mobile game that unwittingly gets you addicted to the word.
Availability:	iTunes & Google Play Stores
Link to View:	http://goo.gl/bygjBi (i-Tunes)
Link to View:	http://goo.gl/F18RM0 (Android)

ABOUT THE AUTHOR

Marricke Kofi Gane, is a gifted African Author, Philosopher, Public Speaker, Coach and Educationist. His writings carry real depth, are highly motivating yet challenging every status quo. He displays dexterity of mind and refined humour where appropriate. He is never shy in some of his works, to show a strong balance between his Christian roots and the reality of living in today's world.

Discover for yourself, all that his writings stand for - to dare, to motivate, to impact!! For more on him, visit www.marrickekofigane.com

Dear Reader,

Thank you for reading this book. I am hopeful that the information provided in it has given you some new learning, challenged you, or provided some answers and inspiration.

I respectfully ask your indulgence in 2 simple ways:

1. Whatever positive action(s) this book has inspired you to take, DO IT NOW. Not later.
2. Help other potential readers who without you, may never read this book by simply following the link below to leave a review. It only takes 3 minutes, but it could be a lifetime blessing for someone out there.

   http://goo.gl/v03bu2

Thank you once again for everything

Marricke Kofi GANE

92428929R10144

Made in the USA
Middletown, DE
08 October 2018